Penguin Books
As I Walked Out One Midsummer Morning

Laurie Lee was born in Gloucester and educated at Slad
village school and at Stroud Central School. At the age of
nineteen he walked to London and then travelled on foot
through Spain, where he was trapped by the outbreak of
the Civil War – to which he later returned by crossing
the Pyrenees (as described in his book *As I Walked Out
One Midsummer Morning*).

During the Second World War he worked for the
Ministry of Information and also made documentary
films in Cyprus and India. In 1950–51 he was Caption-
Writer-in-Chief and Curator of Eccentricities for the
Festival of Britain.

Awarded the M.B.E. in 1952, he has published four
books of poems: *The Sun My Monument* (1944), *The
Bloom of Candles* (1947), *My Many-Coated Man* (1955)
and *Pocket Poems* (1960). His other works include a verse
play for radio, *The Voyage of Magellan* (1948); a record
of his travels in Andalusia, *A Rose for Winter* (1955); his
best-selling autobiography, *Cider with Rosie* (1959), and
its sequel, this book, and *I Can't Stay Long* (1975).

Fond of travelling and music, Laurie Lee finds he works
best in his Chelsea garret, the muddy meadows of Slad,
or certain mountain villages in Spain. He is married and
has a daughter.

Laurie Lee

# *As I Walked Out One Midsummer Morning*

Illustrated by Leonard Rosoman

Penguin Books

Penguin Books Ltd, Harmondsworth,
Middlesex, England
Penguin Books, 625 Madison Avenue,
New York, New York 10022, U.S.A.
Penguin Books Australia Ltd, Ringwood,
Victoria, Australia
Penguin Books Canada, 2801 John Street,
Markham, Ontario, Canada L3R 1B4
Penguin Books (N.Z.) Ltd, 182–190 Wairau Road,
Auckland 10, New Zealand

First published by André Deutsch 1969
First published in the United States of America by
Atheneum Publishers 1969
Published in Penguin Books 1971
Reprinted 1972, 1973, 1974, (twice), 1975, 1976, 1977, 1978, 1979

Made and printed in Great Britain by
Richard Clay (The Chaucer Press) Ltd,
Bungay, Suffolk
Set in Linotype Pilgrim

To T. S. Matthews

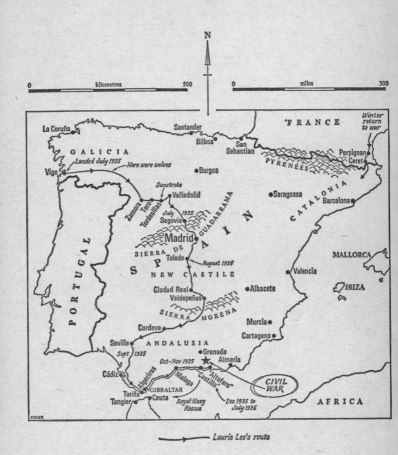

N

| 0 | kilometres | 500 |

| 0 | miles | 300 |

La Coruña
Santander
'F R A N C E
Winter
return
to war

Bilboa

San
Sebastian

G A L I C I A
Here were wolves
Perpignan
Ceret

Landed July 1935
P Y R E N E E S

Vigo
●Burgos

C A T A L O N I A

Sunstroke
●Saragossa

Zamora
Toro
●Valladolid
Barcelona

Tordesillas
July 1935
D E
G U A D A R R A M A

Segovia

S
P
A
I
N

Madrid

P O R T U G A L

SIERRA DE
Toledo
August 1935

MALLORCA

S P A I N

N E W C A S T I L E
●Valencia

Ciudad Real
●Albacete

IBIZA

Valdepeñas
S I E R R A M O R E N A

Cordova
●Murcia

Seville
A N D A L U S I A
Cartagena●

Sept 1935
●Granada
Almeria

Oct-Nov 1935
★

Cádiz
Algeciras
Altofaro
Castillo
CIVIL
WAR

Tarifa
Malaga
Dec 1935 to
July 1936

Tangier
GIBRALTAR
Ceuta
Royal Navy
Rescue
A F R I C A

FISHER

———➤ Laurie Lee's route

# Contents

# 1. London Road

The stooping figure of my mother, waist-deep in the grass and caught there like a piece of sheep's wool, was the last I saw of my country home as I left it to discover the world. She stood old and bent at the top of the bank, silently watching me go, one gnarled red hand raised in farewell and blessing, not questioning why I went. At the bend of the road I looked back again and saw the gold light die behind her; then I turned the corner, passed the village school, and closed that part of my life for ever.

It was a bright Sunday morning in early June, the right time to be leaving home. My three sisters and a brother had already gone before me; two other brothers had yet to make up their minds. They were still sleeping that morning, but my mother had got up early and cooked me a heavy breakfast, had stood wordlessly while I ate it, her hand on my chair, and had then helped me pack up my few belongings. There had been no fuss, no appeals, no attempts at advice or persuasion, only a long and searching look. Then, with my bags on my back, I'd gone out into the early sunshine and climbed through the long wet grass to the road.

It was 1934. I was nineteen years old, still soft at the edges, but with a confident belief in good fortune. I carried a small rolled-up tent, a violin in a blanket, a change of clothes, a tin of treacle biscuits, and some cheese. I was excited, vain-glorious, knowing I had far to go; but not, as yet, how far. As I left home that morning and walked away from the sleeping village, it never occurred to me that others had done this before me.

I was propelled, of course, by the traditional forces that had sent many generations along this road – by the small tight valley closing in around one, stifling the breath with its mossy mouth, the cottage walls narrowing like the arms of an iron maiden, the local girls whispering, 'Marry, and settle down.' Months of restless unease, leading to this inevitable moment, had been spent wandering about the hills, mournfully whist-ling, and watching the high open fields stepping away east-wards under gigantic clouds...

And now I was on my journey, in a pair of thick boots and with a hazel stick in my hand. Naturally, I was going to Lon-don, which lay a hundred miles to the east; and it seemed equally obvious that I should go on foot. But first, as I'd never yet seen the sea, I thought I'd walk to the coast and find it. This would add another hundred miles to my journey, going by way of Southampton. But I had all the summer and all time to spend.

That first day alone – and now I was really alone at last –

steadily declined in excitement and vigour. As I tramped through the dust towards the Wiltshire Downs a growing reluctance weighed me down. White elder-blossom and dog-roses hung in the hedges, blank as unwritten paper, and the hot empty road – there were few motor cars then – reflected Sunday's waste and indifference. High sulky summer sucked me towards it, and I offered no resistance at all. Through the solitary morning and afternoon I found myself longing for some opposition or rescue, for the sound of hurrying footsteps coming after me and family voices calling me back.

None came. I was free. I was affronted by freedom. The day's silence said, Go where you will. It's all yours. You asked for it. It's up to you now. You're on your own, and nobody's going to stop you. As I walked, I was taunted by echoes of home, by the tinkling sounds of the kitchen, shafts of sun from the windows falling across the familiar furniture, across the bedroom and the bed I had left.

When I judged it to be tea-time I sat on an old stone wall and opened my tin of treacle biscuits. As I ate them I could hear mother banging the kettle on the hob and my brothers rattling their tea-cups. The biscuits tasted sweetly of the honeyed squalor of home – still only a dozen miles away.

I might have turned back then if it hadn't been for my brothers, but I couldn't have borne the look on their faces. So I got off the wall and went on my way. The long evening shadows pointed to folded villages, homing cows, and after-church walkers. I tramped the edge of the road, watching my dusty feet, not stopping again for a couple of hours.

When darkness came, full of moths and beetles, I was too weary to put up the tent. So I lay myself down in the middle of a field and stared up at the brilliant stars. I was oppressed by the velvety emptiness of the world and the swathes of soft grass I lay on. Then the fumes of the night finally put me to sleep – my first night without a roof or bed.

I was woken soon after midnight by drizzling rain on my face, the sky black and the stars all gone. Two cows stood over me, windily sighing, and the wretchedness of that moment haunts me still. I crawled into a ditch and lay awake till dawn, soaking alone in that nameless field. But when the sun rose in the morning the feeling of desolation was over. Birds sang, and the grass steamed warmly. I got up and shook myself, ate a piece of cheese, and turned again to the south.

Now I came down through Wiltshire, burning my roots behind me and slowly getting my second wind; taking it easy, idling through towns and villages, and knowing what it was like not to have to go to work. Four years as a junior in that gaslit office in Stroud had kept me pretty closely tied. Now I was tasting the extravagant quality of being free on a weekday, say at eleven o'clock in the morning, able to scuff down a side-road and watch a man herding sheep, or a stalking cat in the grass, or to beg a screw of tea from a housewife and carry it into a wood and spend an hour boiling a can of spring water.

As for this pocket of England through which I found myself walking, it seemed to me immense. A motor car, of course, could have crossed it in a couple of hours, but it took me the best part of a week, treading it slowly, smelling its different soils, spending a whole morning working round a hill. I was lucky, I know, to have been setting out at that time, in a landscape not yet bulldozed for speed. Many of the country roads still followed their original tracks, drawn by packhorse or lumbering cartwheel, hugging the curve of a valley or yielding to a promontory like the wandering line of a stream. It was not, after all, so very long ago, but no one could make that journey today. Most of the old roads have gone, and the motor car, since then, has begun to cut the landscape to pieces, through which the hunched-up traveller races at gutter height, seeing less than a dog in a ditch.

But for me, at that time, everything I saw was new, and I could pass it slowly through the hours of the day. While still only a day's march from home, coming through Malmesbury and Chippenham, already I noticed different shades of speech. Then a day or so later I passed down the Wylye Valley and came out on to a vast and rolling plain – a sweep of old dry land covered with shaggy grass which looked as though it had just been cropped by mammoths. Still vague about places, I was unprepared for the delicate spire that rose suddenly out of the empty plain. As I walked, it went before me, gliding behind the curve of the hill and giving no hint of the city beneath it.

Just a spire in the grass; my first view of Salisbury, and the better for not being expected. When I entered the city I found it was market day, the square crowded with bone-thin sheep. Farmers stood round in groups talking sideways to each other and all looking in opposite directions. The pubs were bursting with dealers counting out crumpled money. Shepherds and dogs sat around on the pavements. Supreme above all towered the misty cathedral, still prince of the horizontal town, throwing its slow shifting shade across the market square and jingling handfuls of bells like coins.

After a week on the road I finally arrived at Southampton, where I'd been told I would see the sea. Instead, I saw a few rusty cranes and a compressed looking liner wedged tightly between some houses; also some sad allotments fringing a muddy river which they said was Southampton Water.

Southampton Town, on the other hand, came up to all expectations, proving to be salty and shifty in turns, like some ship-jumping sailor who'd turned his back on the sea in a desperate attempt to make good on land. The streets near the water appeared to be jammed with shops designed more for entertainment than profit, including tattooists, ear-piercers, bump-readers, fortune-tellers, whelk-bars, and pudding boilers. There were also shops selling kites and Chinese paper dragons, coloured sands and tropical birds; and lots of little step-down taverns panelled with rum-soaked timbers and reeking of pickled eggs and onions.

As I'd been sleeping in fields for a week, I thought it was time I tried a bed again, so I went to a doss-house down by the docks. The landlady, an old hag with a tooth like a tin-opener, said it would cost me a shilling a night, demanded the money in advance, treated me to a tumblerful of whisky, then showed me up to the attic.

Early next morning she brought me a cup of tea and some water in a wooden bucket. She looked at me vaguely and asked what ship I was from, and only grunted when I said I'd come from Stroud. Then she spotted my violin hanging on the end of the bed and gave it a twang with her long blue nails.

'Well, hey diddle diddle, I reckon,' she muttered, and skipped nimbly out of the room.

Presently I got up and dressed, stuck my violin under my jacket, and went out into the streets to try my luck. It was now or never. I must face it now, or pack up and go back home. I wandered about for an hour looking for a likely spot, feeling as though I were about to commit a crime. Then I stopped at last under a bridge near the station and decided to have a go.

I felt tense and shaky. It was the first time, after all. I drew the violin from my coat like a gun. It was here, in Southampton, with trains rattling overhead, that I was about to declare myself. One moment I was part of the hurrying crowds, the next I stood nakedly apart, my back to the wall, my hat on the pavement before me, the violin under my chin.

The first notes I played were loud and raw, like a hoarse declaration of protest, then they settled down and began to run more smoothly and to stay more or less in tune. To my surprise, I was neither arrested nor told to shut up. Indeed, nobody took any notice at all. Then an old man, without stopping, surreptitiously tossed a penny into my hat as though getting rid of some guilty evidence.

Other pennies followed, slowly but steadily, dropped by shadows who appeared not to see or hear me. It was as though the note of the fiddle touched some subconscious nerve that had to be answered – like a baby's cry. When I'd finished the first tune there was over a shilling in my hat : it seemed too easy, like a confidence trick. But I was elated now; I felt that wherever I went from here this was a trick I could always live by.

I worked the streets of Southampton for several days, gradually acquiring the truths of the trade. Obvious enough to old-timers, and simple, once learnt, I had to get them by trial and error. It was not a good thing, for instance, to let the hat fill up with money – the sight could discourage the patron; nor was it wise to empty it completely, which could also confuse him, giving him no hint as to where to drop his money. Placing a couple of pennies in the hat to start the thing going soon became an unvarying ritual; making sure, between tunes, to take off the cream, but always leaving two pennies behind.

Slow melodies were best, encouraging people to dawdle (Irish jigs sent them whizzing past); but it also seemed wise to play as well as one was able rather than to ape the dirge of the professional waif. To arouse pity or guilt was always good for a penny, but that was as far as it got you; while a tuneful appeal to the ear, played with sober zest, might often be rewarded with silver.

Old ladies were most generous, and so were women with children, shopgirls, typists, and barmaids. As for the men: heavy drinkers were always receptive, so were big chaps with muscles, bookies, and punters. But never a man with a bowler, briefcase, or dog; respectable types were the tightest of all. Except for retired army officers, who would bark, 'Why aren't you working, young man?' and then over-tip to hide their confusion.

Certain tunes, I discovered, always raised a response, while others touched off nothing at all. The most fruitful were invariably the tea-room classics and certain of the juicier national ballads. 'Loch Lomond', 'Wales! Wales!', and 'The Rose of Tralee' called up their supporters from any crowd – as did 'Largo', 'Ave Maria', Toselli's 'Serenade', and 'The Whistler and His Dog'. The least rewarding, as I said, was anything quick or flashy, such as 'The Devil's Trill' or 'Picking up Sticks', which seemed to throw the pedestrian right out of his stride and completely shatter his charitable rhythm.

All in all, my apprenticeship proved profitable and easy, and I soon lost my pavement nerves. It became a greedy pleasure to go out into the streets, to take up my stand by the station or market, and start sawing away at some moony melody and watch the pennies and halfpennies grow. Those first days in Southampton were a kind of obsession; I was out in the streets from morning till night, moving from pitch to pitch in a gold-dust fever, playing till the tips of my fingers burned.

When I judged Southampton to have taken about as much as it could, I decided to move on eastwards. Already I felt like a

veteran, and on my way out of town I went into a booth to
have my photograph taken. The picture was developed in a
bucket in less than a minute, and has lasted over thirty years. I
still have a copy before me of that summer ghost – a pale,
oleaginous shade, posed daintily before a landscape of tattered
canvas, his old clothes powdered with dust. He wears a sloppy
slouch hat, heavy boots, baggy trousers, tent and fiddle slung
over his shoulders, and from the long empty face gaze a pair of
egg-shell eyes, unhatched, and unrecognizable now.

A few miles from Southampton I saw the real sea at last, head
on, a sudden end to the land, a great sweep of curved nothing
rolling out to the invisible horizon and revealing more distance
than I'd ever seen before. It was green, and heaved gently like
the skin of a frog, and carried drowsy little ships like flies.
Compared with the land, it appeared to be a huge hypnotic
blank, putting everything to sleep that touched it.

As I pushed along the shore I was soon absorbed by its atmosphere, new, mysterious, alien : the gritty edge on the wind,
the taste of tar and salt, the smell of stale sea-shells, damp roads,
and mackintoshes, and the sight of the quick summer storms
sliding in front of the water like sheets of dirty glass.

The South Coast, even so, was not what I'd been led to expect – from reading Hardy and Jeffery Farnol – for already it
had begun to develop that shabby shoreline suburbia which
was part of the whimsical rot of the Thirties. Here were the sea-
shanty-towns, sprawled like a rubbishy tidemark, the scattered litter of land and ocean – miles of tea-shacks and bunga-
lows, apparently built out of wreckage, and called 'Spindrift'
or 'Sprite O' The Waves'. Here and there, bearded men sat on
broken verandas painting water-colours of boats and sunsets,
while big women with dogs, all glistening with teeth, policed
parcels of private sand. I liked the seedy disorder of this melancholy coast, unvisited as yet by prosperity, and looking as
though everything about it had been thrown together by the
winds, and might at any moment be blown away again.

I spent a week by the sea, slowly edging towards the east,
sleeping on the shore and working the towns. I remember it as

a blur of summer, indolent and vague, broken occasionally by some odd encounter. At Gosport I performed at a barrack-room concert in return for a ration of army beef. In front of Chichester Cathedral I played 'Bless this House', and was moved on at once by the police. At Bognor Regis I camped out on the sands where I met a fluid young girl of sixteen, who hugged me steadily throughout one long hot day with only a gymslip on her sea-wet body. At Littlehampton, I'd just collected about eighteen pence when I was moved on again by the police. 'Not here. Try Worthing,' the officer said. I did so, and was amply rewarded.

Worthing at that time was a kind of Cheltenham-on-Sea, full of rich, pearl-chokered invalids. Each afternoon they came out in their high-wheeled chairs and were pushed round the park by small hired men. Standing at the gate of the park, in the mainstream of these ladies, I played a selection of spiritual airs, and in little over an hour collected thirty-eight shillings – which was more than a farm-labourer earned in a week.

Worthing was an end to that chapter, a junction in the journey, and as far along the coast as I wished to go. So I turned my back on the sea and headed north for London, still over fifty miles away. It was the third week in June, and the landscape was frosty with pollen and still coated with elder-blossom. The wide-open Downs, the sheep-nibbled grass, the beech hangers on the edge of the valleys, the smell of chalk, purple orchids, blue butterflies, and thistles recalled the Cotswolds I'd so carelessly left. Indeed Chanctonbury Ring, where I slept that night, could have been any of the beacons round Painswick or Haresfield; yet I felt farther from home, by the very familiarity of my surroundings, than I ever did later in a foreign country.

But next day, getting back on to the London road, I forgot everything but the way ahead. I walked steadily, effortlessly, hour after hour, in a kind of swinging, weightless dream. I was at that age which feels neither strain nor friction, when the body burns magic fuels, so that it seems to glide in warm air, about a foot off the ground, smoothly obeying its intuitions. Even exhaustion, when it came, had a voluptuous quality, and sleep was caressive and deep, like oil. It was the peak of the curve of the body's total extravagance, before the accounts start coming in.

I was living at that time on pressed dates and biscuits, rationing them daily, as though crossing a desert. Sussex, of course, offered other diets, but I preferred to stick to this affectation. I pretended I was T. E. Lawrence, engaged in some self-punishing odyssey, burning up my youth in some pitless Hadhramaut, eyes narrowing to the sandstorms blowing out of the wadis of Godalming in a mirage of solitary endurance.

But I was not the only one on the road; I soon noticed there were many others, all trudging northwards in a sombre procession. Some, of course, were professional tramps, but the majority belonged to that host of unemployed who wandered aimlessly about England at that time.

One could pick out the professionals; they brewed tea by the roadside, took it easy, and studied their feet. But the others, the majority, went on their way like somnambulists, walking alone and seldom speaking to each other. There seemed to be more of them inland than on the coast – maybe the police had seen to that. They were like a broken army walking away from a war, cheeks sunken, eyes dead with fatigue. Some carried bags of tools, or shabby cardboard suitcases; some wore the ghosts of city suits; some, when they stopped to rest, carefully removed their shoes and polished them vaguely with handfuls of grass. Among them were carpenters, clerks, engineers from the Midlands; many had been on the road for months, walking up and down the country in a maze of jobless refusals, the treadmill of the mid-Thirties ...

Then, for a couple of days, I got a companion. I was picked up by the veteran Alf. I'd turned off the road to set up camp for the night, when he came filtering through the bushes.

I'd seen him before; he was about five feet high and was clearly one of the brotherhood. He wore a deerstalker hat, so sodden and shredded it looked like a helping of breakfast food, and round the waist of his mackintosh, which was belted with string, hung a collection of pots and spoons.

Rattling like a dustbin, he sat down beside me and began pulling off his boots.

'Well,' he said, eyeing my dates with disgust, 'you're a poor little bleeder, 'ent you?'

He shook out his boots and put them on again, then gave my supper another look.

'You can't live on terrible tack like that – you'll depress the lot of us. What you want is a billy. A-boil yerself up. 'Ere, 'ang on – jus' wait a minute . . .'

Rummaging through the hardware around his waist, he produced a battered can, the kind of thing my uncles brought home from the war – square, with a triangular handle. It was a miniature cauldron, smoke-blackened outside and dark, tannin-stained within.

' 'Ere, take it,' he said. 'You make me miserable.' He started to build a fire. 'I'm goin' to boil you a bit of tea and tatters.' And that is what he did.

We stayed together as far as Guildford, and I shared more of his pungent brews. He was a tramp to his bones, always wrapping and unwrapping himself, and picking over his bits and pieces. He wasn't looking for work; this was simply his life, and he carefully rationed his energies – never passing a patch of grass that looked good for a shakedown, nor a cottage that seemed ripe for charity. He said his name was Alf, but one couldn't be sure, as he called me Alf, and everyone else. 'Couple of Alfs got jugged in this town last year,' he'd say. 'Hookin' the shops – you know, with fish-hooks.' Or: 'An Alf I knew used to do twenty-mile a day. One of the looniest Alfs on the road. Said he got round it quicker. And so he did. But folks got sick of his face.'

Alf talked all day, but was garrulously secretive, and never revealed his origins. I suppose that in the shared exposure of the open road he needed this loose verbal hedge around him. At the same time, he never asked me about myself, though he took it for granted that I was a greenhorn, and gave me careful advice about insulation from weather, flannelling housewives, and dodging the cops.

As for his own technique of roadwork, he wasn't slow out of

laziness but because he moved to a deliberate timetable, making his professional grand tour in a twelve-months' rhythm, which seemed to him fast enough. During the winter he'd hole up in a London doss-house, then restart his leisurely cycle of England, turning up every year in each particular district with the regularity of the seasons. Thus he was the spring tramp of the Midlands, the summer bird of the south, the first touch of autumn to the Kentish Weald – indeed, I think he firmly believed that his constancy of motion spread a kind of reassurance among the housewives, so that he was looked for and welcomed as one of the recurring phenomena of nature, and was suitably rewarded therefore.

Certainly his begging was profitable, and he never popped through a gate without returning with fistfuls of food – screws of tea, sugar, meat bones, and cake, which he'd then boil in one awful mess. He was clean, down-at-heel, warm-hearted, and cunning; and he showed me genuine if supercilious kindness. 'You're a bleedin' disgrace,' he used to say, 'a miserable little burden.'

Alf had one strange habit – a passion for nursery rhymes, which he'd mutter as he walked along.

> Sing a song of sixpence,
> Pocketful of rye,
> Four-an'-twenny blackbirds
> Baked in an oven.
>
> Ba-ba, black sheep,
> Have you any wool?
> Yes, sir, yes, sir,
> I got plenty ...

The effect of a dozen of these, left hanging in the air, was enough to dislocate the senses.

At Guildford we parted, Alf turning east for the Weald, which for him still lay three months away.

'So long, Alf,' I said.

'So long, Alf,' he answered. 'Try not to be too much of a nuisance.'

He passed under the railway bridge and out of my life, a shuffling rattle of old tin cans, looking very small and triangular with his pointed hat on his head, and black mackintosh trailing the ground.

London was now quite near, not more than a two-days' walk, but I was still in no particular hurry. So I turned north-west and began a detour round it, rather like a wasp sidling up to a jam jar. After leaving Guildford, I slept on Bagshot Heath – all birches, sand, and horseflies – which to me seemed a sinister and wasted place like some vast dead land of Russia. Then next morning, only a few miles farther up the road, everything suddenly changed back again, and I was walking through parkland as green as a fable, smothered with beeches and creamy grass.

Every motor car on the road was now either a Rolls-Royce or a Daimler – a gliding succession of silver sighs – their crystal interiors packed with girls and hampers and erect top-hatted men. Previously, I'd not seen more than two such cars in my life; now they seemed to be the only kind in the world, and I began to wonder if they were intimations of treasures to come, whether all London was as rich as this.

Tramping in the dust of this splendour, I wasn't surprised when one of the Daimlers pulled up and an arm beckoned to me from the window. I hurried towards it, thinking it might be full of long-lost relations, but in fact there was no one I knew. 'Want a pheasant, my man?' asked a voice from inside. 'We just knocked over a beauty a hundred yards back.'

A quarter of an hour later I arrived at Ascot. It was race week, and I'd walked right into it. White pavilions and flags; little grooms and jockeys dodging among the long glossy legs of thoroughbreds; and the pedigree owners dipping their long cool necks into baskets of paté and gulls' eggs.

I went round to the entrance, thinking I might get in, but was stared at by a couple of policemen. So I stared, in turn, at a beautiful woman by the gate, who for a moment paused dazz-

lingly near me – her face as silkily finished as a Persian miniature, her body sheathed in swathes like a tulip, and her san-
dalled feet wrapped in a kind of transparent rice-paper so that I
could count every clean little separate toe.

Wealth and beauty were the common order of things now,
and I felt I had entered another realm. It would have been no
good busking or touting here, indeed outlandish in such a
place. Alf, and the tattered lines of the workless, were far away
in another country ... So I left Ascot, and came presently to
another park, full of oak trees and grazing deer, and saw Wind-
sor Castle standing on its green-baize hill like a battered silver
cruet. I slept that stifling night in a field near Stoke Poges,
having spent the evening in the village churchyard, sitting on a
mossy gravestone and listening to the rooks, and wondering
why the place seemed so familiar.

A few mornings later, coming out of a wood near Beaconsfield,
I suddenly saw London at last – a long smoky skyline hazed by
the morning sun and filling the whole of the eastern horizon.
Dry, rusty-red, it lay like a huge flat crust, like ash from some
spent volcano, simmering gently in the summer morning and
emitting a faint, metallic roar.

No architectual glories, no towers or palaces, just a creeping
insidious presence, its vast horizontal broken here and there by
a gasholder or factory chimney. Even so, I could already feel
its intense radiation – an electric charge in the sky – that rose
from its million roofs in a quivering mirage, magnetically, almost visibly, dilating.

Cleo, my girl-friend, was somewhere out there; hoarding my
letters (I hoped) and waiting. Also mystery, promise, chance,
and fortune – all I had come to this city to find. I hurried
towards it, impatient now, its sulphur stinging my nostrils. I
had been a month on the road, and the suburbs were long and
empty. In the end I took a tube.

# 2. London

My village, my home-town, each had a kind of duck-pond centre, but London had no centre at all – just squat little streets endlessly proliferating themselves like ripples in estuary mud. I arrived at Paddington in the early evening, and walked around for a while. The sky was different here, high, wide, and still, rosy with smoke, and the westering sun. There was a smell of rank oil, rotting fish and vegetables, hot pavements and trodden tar; and a sense of surging pressure, the heavy used-up air of the cheek-by-jowl life around me – the families fermenting behind slack-coloured curtains, above shops and in resounding tenements, sons changing their shirts, daughters drying their hair, waistcoated fathers staring at their tea, and in the streets the packed buses grinding nose to tail and the great night coming on.

I was excited, having got here, but also unprepared, and I wasn't sure what I was going to do. But I had Cleo's address – I didn't know anyone else – so I thought this was the time to use it. I'd met Cleo in the spring, in a Tolstoyan settlement near Stroud, where she was living in a borrowed caravan, together with her handsome father – an eagle-nosed left-wing agitator – and her distressed and well-born mother.

Their origins were uncertain, but they'd recently fled from America, where I suspect the father had been in some political trouble. The sixteen-year-old girl was not the kind I'd been used to, and her beauty had knocked me silly. She'd had a husky, nutty Anglo-American accent, huge brown eyes flecked like crumbled honey, a smooth leggy figure, lithe as an Indian pony; and we'd pretended to be in love.

The family were penniless, but they had connections, and friends were always lending them houses; and the address of the last one – somewhere on Putney Heath – sounded very grand indeed. When I finally got there, having walked several miles through the dusk, the house appeared to have been hit by a bomb – only half a wing and the main staircase still standing in a huge garden of churned-up roots.

They were sitting on the staircase, which was open to the sky, and seemed rather surprised to see me – except for lovely Cleo, who cried 'I knew it!' and ran down the steps to meet me. She had kept up superbly with my memories of her, and looked even better than I expected, her body packed beautifully into her shirt and shorts, and her skin the colour of rosewood.

'You walked it, didn't you? – I *told* you, Daddy.' She led me proudly up the eroded staircase, then took me to her room and showed me my bundle of letters which lay wrapped in her scented nightdress.

So I was invited to stay. Cleo burnt my clothes and fitted me out with some of her father's. The mansion was being torn down to make room for a block of flats, and the father had a job with the builders; meanwhile, with the half-ruin to live in, they were temporarily secure, and the mother was slowly recovering her senses.

I slept on the floor in the remaining fragment of ballroom, and ate with the family in the Victorian kitchen, whose tall Gothic windows looked from the lip of the Heath across London to the Hampstead hills. I was in luck, and I knew it, and took it easy at first. It seemed a nice soft spot to be in. Sometimes the father, in his loud public voice, would lecture me on the theory of anarchy, on the necessity for political and personal freedom, and on his contempt for the moral law. When he was out, the mother, pale and damp round the eyes, would talk about her childhood home in the shires, and lament the scruffy world of conspiratorial garrets through which this attractive bounder had led her. At other times the daughter, heart-stoppingly voluptuous in her tight Californian pants, would lead me by the hand through the ruined garden, to the last clump of still-rooted myrtles, then crouch, bare-kneed, and pull me down beside her, and demand to know my ideological convictions.

Beautiful Cleo; she never knew what she did to me, her eyes slanting under the myrtle leaves, her coiled russet limbs like something from a Rousseau jungle, her chatter never still for a moment. But not of what I expected; never a word about love, or my hunger, or the summer night. The funeral baked meats of her father's mind were all she seemed able to serve me. He was the one, of course, and I was not old enough to replace him. I thought her the most ravishing and wasted child in the world.

Then one night I took her out on to the twilit Heath, where lovers lay thick as sheaves. We walked miles round the common, and Cleo never drew breath; her lovely mouth was a political megaphone. Finally I pushed her against a tree and desperately kissed her. She lent me her lips like an improving book. 'But I *must* have the Movement. You understand, don't you? You *must* join the Party,' she said.

I didn't give up. I made one last try. After all, I was in considerable torment. So next morning, at dawn, I fetched one of the builder's ladders and climbed through her bedroom window. She lay easily sleeping in her rose-coloured night-dress, a soft breathing heap of love. The hushed dawn, the first birds, and me in my black Russian pyjamas – surely she must melt to this magic moment. As I slipped into her bed she rolled drowsily into my arms, then woke, and her body froze. 'If Daddy knew about this, he'd murder you,' she said. It was no idle figure of speech.

Scrambling back down the ladder in the dawn's early light, I realized that blood could be thicker than theory. Later that day, Cleo's father got me a job with the builders, and gave me the address of some Putney lodgings. I don't know what she had told him, but he'd acted swiftly. It seemed a reasonable compromise between New Thought and the horsewhip.

On my own once again, I found a snug little room over an eating-house in the Lower Richmond Road – a shambling second-floor back which overhung the railway and rocked all day to the passing trains, while the hot meaty steam of boiling pies filtered up through cracks in the floor.

The café downstairs was a shadowy tunnel lined with high-backed wooden pews, carbolic-scrubbed and exclusively male, with all the comforts of a medieval refectory. My rent of twenty-five shillings a week included the furnished room and three café meals a day – a *carte blanche* arrangement which I exploited fully and which introduced me to new ways of eating. The blackboard menu, propped on the pavement outside, offered a list as immutable as the elements: 'Bubble. Squeak. Liver and B. Toad-in-the-Hole. Meat Pudding or Pie.' My favourite was the pie – a little basin of meat wrapped in a caul of suety dough which was kept boiling all day in a copper cauldron in a cupboard under the stairs. Turned out on the plate, it steamed like a sodden napkin, emitting a mournful odour of laundries; but once pricked with the fork it exploded magnificently with a rich lava of beefy juices. There must have been over a pound of meat in each separate pie – a complete working-man's meal, for sixpence. And remembering the thin days at home, when meat was only for Sundays, I ate at least one of them every day. Otherwise I was encouraged to ring the changes on the house's limited permutations – Squeak, Toad, Liver and B; or as a privilege, an occasional herring. A mug of tea at each meal was of course served without asking, and was so strong you could trot a mouse on it. As for afters, there was a postscript at the foot of the menu which seemed to be painted in permanent enamel: 'During the Present Hot Spell Why Not Try a Cold Sweet?' Winter and summer, it was custard and prunes.

Arnold, the proprietor – who was also my landlord – was a man in his early thirties, a rounded dandy with heavy cream-white jowls and delicate parboiled hands. He did all the work alone, both the cooking and serving, and moved with the rolling dignity of a eunuch, dressed in tight cotton gowns, buttoned up to the throat, which also gave him the appearance of one of his cloth-wrapped pies. He was bald, large-headed, red-lipped and corseted, and was given to abstractions, silence and reveries; and he seemed clearly to be a cut above his clients, though if he thought so, he never showed it. Each day, before breakfast, he padded around the tables laying out the morning newspapers like hymn-sheets; and these again were scrupulously changed in the evening. The customers also had the benefit of his soft-voiced summaries. I've never known a man who gave to this particular job such a sense of modest almost priest-like dedication, advising and serving the labourers at his table and taking their coppers like a church collection.

In fact, this ascetic purveyor of gross Toads and Squeaks was something of a mystery. One might have imagined him to have chosen the job as a purge, an act of self-abasement; but certainly not for the money. I lived for six months in his house, but I never knew him – though I knew he had another life. I knew, for instance, about the two pretty children who visited him briefly each Saturday night. And that in his first-floor back he kept in careful seclusion a young and beautiful wife. Sometimes as I climbed to my room, I saw her standing in her half-open doorway, a tantalizing strip of voluptuous boredom, her hair piled high and elaborately set, her eyes burning like landing lights. She wore a white silk wrap buttoned up to the throat, and her toe-nails were painted green. She was about my own age, but she never spoke. Nor did Arnold ever mention her.

My job at the buildings took it out of me at first, and I lived at a pitch of healthy exhaustion. All day I pushed barrows of wet cement till my muscles stretched and burned. At night, I returned to the steaming café, ate my pie, then climbed to my backstairs room, where I sat half-dozing at the window table, gazing down at the long green trains.

It was the first time in my life I'd had a room of my own, uncluttered with sisters and brothers, and I spread all over it, throwing my clothes about, and keeping the door well locked and bolted. Grateful for privacy at last, I was content just to sit there, lord of the room and its chromium furniture, spending the long summer evenings nodding alone at the table, or drawing girls, or writing short sleepy poems. London waited outside – a stubby plateau of chimneys, a low mutter of dragging sound; but at the beginning there was little I could do about it. My body was too used up.

It took a little while to get toughened-up to the job, to the stiff hours of blistering labour, which wore my hands into holes and pulled my muscles about into new and unaccustomed contortions. I was dead-beat at first, and walked in a tottering daze; but I was young, and I hardened fast. Soon my palms had calluses rough as salted leather, which I could rub together with pride. At last I could get home in the evening without falling into a stupor. I could even begin to look about me.

Of course, I'd not much identity with the city yet; it was just rooftops and a changing sky, a thump of radios coming from open windows, and the summer yelp of the back-street children. And the frail cord with my family was still uncut. Boot-boxes of flowers came by post from my mother, sweet slipshod gatherings from the fields and hedges, wrapped in damp moss and ivy leaves.

Then I made a small break-through. I won a poetry prize in a weekly competition organized by a newspaper, *The Sunday Referee* – for a poem I'd dashed off with a sixpenny postal order

and never expected to hear of again. Arnold showed it to me
one morning, his red mouth twitching; and it was the first of
mine I'd ever seen printed. 'Is this really you?' he asked fastidiously. 'I wasn't aware you had such beautiful thoughts.'

Soon after this, I met Philip O'Connor distributing leaflets on
Putney Common – a quick ready youth with a fine hungry face
and a shock of thick obsidian curls. We were both of us living
alone at that time, scribbling poetry in neighbouring streets, so
for a while we visited each other quite often, establishing a
defensive minority of two. To me, he had an adolescent mystery about him, a frenetic melancholy, like a schoolboy Hamlet;
and his poems were the most extravagant I'd read until then,
rhapsodic eruptions of surrealist fantasy. I was impressed by
his poems; he thought little of mine. I was the older; he was
paternal. He used to lie on my bed, nervously scratching his
curls, and switching his dark eyes on and off, reciting his latest
verses in clear cold tones, snappy and rather bitter. 'You and I
are the only true voices left alive in the world,' he'd say. When
using my room, his manners were perfect. Not so on his own
home ground, when his claims were more self-centred. But he
had a nice sense of territory.

Another friend of that period was six-foot Billy, who ate
regularly in the café downstairs – a stranded Negro sailor from
Troy, Missouri, who had either jumped ship or had lost his
way. I never knew where he slept, or how he lived, but every
evening he'd be there in his pew, dropping great lumps of
butter into his hot strong tea and carefully stripping the bones
from a kipper. His huge fat cheeks were lightly scarred by
knives, and the marks of knuckledusters ran across his eyebrows. But he was sleepily gentle, never raised his voice, and
his favourite diversions seemed to be tea and gossip. Billy was
an excellent listener, and it seemed impossible to bore him.
He'd salute the dullest story with the most flattering attention.
'Waal, ah'll go slash mah wrists, if that ain't sumpin',' he'd
murmur. 'You may hang me up by mah entrails.' Sometimes
he'd disappear for a few days, then pop up, beaming. 'Gouge
mah eyes, shuh good to see you.' Then we'd go next door for a
game of billiards, which he played with a velvet touch. But he

didn't last long. They finally caught up with him. A dozen coppers with rolled-up macs. Stepping gingerly into the café, expecting a struggle. But he went with them like a child.

Then my days with Arnold, too, were numbered. A girl came to live on the floor above me. She moved into the attic cupboard just under the roof, which till then had only stored potatoes. The girl seemed to do no work, though occasionally I'd hear her gramophone playing and the sound of her bare feet dancing. Sometimes we'd meet on the stairs and have to struggle together to get round the bend in the banisters. A couple of inches from mine, her eyes never blinked. Her hair smelt of pies and doughnuts. 'D'you see that film called *The Rat*?' she asked me one day. 'You're his bleedin' image, you are.' Her friends came in the evening, and left in the morning. Then Arnold would take her breakfast up on a tray. At last, apologetically, he said he'd be wanting my room. It seemed he was extending the business.

The next lodging I found was somewhat more secure, with a half-Cockney, half-Irish family, who lived in a compact little set-up a dozen yards from the High Street in a squat row of Victorian villas. Here, for twenty-five shillings a week, I got a ground-floor room, meals and laundry and a bright coal fire, the use of the parlour on Sundays, and the warmth of the basement kitchen whenever I felt like extra company.

Mrs Flynn, my landlady, was a valiant blonde, with something of the twilight beauty of Gloria Swanson – a kind of smooth open face that was tough yet wistful, backed by a garrulous and romantic fancy. There seemed to be two Mrs Flynns: one girlish and easy, the other born to furious protest. Mornings saw her most angry, a chain-smoking sweeper of rooms, a tousled mop in a dressing-gown; then at night, after supper, she emerged in laminated gold, with silkily reconditioned hair, to engage the world in a monologue of bubbling non-sequiturs, full of giggles, regrets, and yearnings. Sleekly bent to her cocoa, splendidly robed and corseted, she would then tackle any subject on earth. She'd describe the deer out at Richmond, wearing their beautiful antelopes. She'd give her views on the Russian revulsion. She'd warn me never to get married; she'd married too young, a mistake, she'd been much too impressive. But she liked men with thick lips, the curling rose-bud type – she always thought they looked so essential . . .

Mrs Flynn was Cockney, her absent husband Irish. But there was another somewhere lost in her life. He had been Irish too, a Celtic prince, now gone. She'd mention him tragically, then hoot with laughter. It was that robust, good-natured hunger about her that balanced her bouts of frenzy. Together with those easy tears and sudden giggles of self-mockery. She must have been younger than I thought at the time.

The rest of the family consisted of Mrs Flynn's two children, who were as different as night from day – black-eyed Patsy, a sexily confident child of eight, and blond Mike, a speechless lad of eleven. There was also Beth, the landlady's unmarried sister, a fey, self-effacing spirit, who moved in the background like an anxious guardian and held the whole house together. She watched over us all, worked in an office by day, cooked the supper and scrubbed clothes in the evening, reflected her sister's moods like a seismograph, and shyly explained and excused. The women were much alike, though Beth was the older and took pains to conceal the likeness, having suppressed her own beauty, like a nerve-failed actress, to become her sister's dresser and shadow.

I soon fitted into the house, and was enveloped by it. My room was small, just the kind I prefer. There was a bed, a chair, a coloured print of Killarney, and a barred window looking out on a wall. With winter coming on, I could have done much worse. The place was snug as a badger's hole. And the women treated me well, like a fragile exotic, as though fattening me up for a prize. In the morning young Mike brought me breakfast in bed, together with a fat wad of sandwiches for work. When I returned in the evening the coal fire was blazing and the room whirling with sulphurous smoke. At six, a huge meal on a copper tray was brought in by the pigtailed Patsy, who then sat on the floor, her bare knees to her chin, and mercilessly watched me eat. She'd pay another brief visit before going to bed. 'Ma says anything else you want?' Squirming, coy, a strip of striped pyjamas, Miss Sweater Girl of ten years later – already she knew how to stand, how to snuggle against the doorpost, how to frame her flannel-dressed limbs in the lamplight.

Once the children were in bed, other sounds took over, mysterious but soon familiar. Beth down at the sink, mangling the evening's wash or chopping up piles of sandwiches for the morning. Mrs Flynn, in pale fur, leaving for the Wembley dogs, or stranded alone for the night in the basement, banging her head on the table or laughing the whole thing off with a half-pint bottle of stout. Then sometimes, quite late, from away in the attic, one might hear a succession of howls and groans, reverberating alarms pitched in a sepulchral baritone like the complaining of Hamlet's ghost. But it was only Mr Willow, Mrs Flynn's other lodger, an old actor long since retired, who liked to fill up his solitude by repeating the lines of his one-time triumph: *The Curse of Dr Fu Manchu.*

Otherwise, when home, I spent self-contained evenings, writing by the fire, or playing the fiddle, till just before bed Beth brought me a large tray of supper and perhaps something she'd copied for me to read. It was like being in a family again, except that these knocked on my door and didn't ask me to help with the house work. And when I was ill they looked after me, reduced the rent, and Mrs Flynn brought me bottles of Guinness. 'That Laurie,' she'd say. 'No wonder he goes like that. He burdens his brain too much.' She didn't know much about me, nor did she try to find out. It seemed enough that I made a change.

As for the great spread of London, which I'd come to discover, I don't think I even began to get the feel of it then. Its dimensions were all wrong for my country-grown mind, too out-of-scale for my experience to cope with. In any case I was twenty, when environment plays tricks, and my portholes were fogged by illusion. I just floated around in a capsule of self-absorption, sealed in with my own private weather.

But I can remember the presence of London, its physical toughness at that time, its home-spun, knock-about air. There was more life in the streets (it cost money inside) and people thronged outdoors in the evenings. One saw them standing on corners, in the doorways of pubs, talking in groups, eating from paper bags. And the streets themselves had an almost rustic confusion – Edwardian transport in all its last-ditch vigour: rattling old buses, coster ponies and traps, prim little taxis like upright pianos, and huge dray wagons laden with beer and flour and drawn by teams of magnificent horses. Then of fine Sunday mornings, while the horses rested, Putney High Street filled up with bicycles – buxom girls in white shorts chased by puffing young men, old straw-hatted gents in blazers, whole families on tandems carrying their babies in baskets, and all heading for the open country. Private cars were few, and were often a sign of ill-omen, particularly when parked in a side street, where the sight of a car outside a terraced house might well mean the doctor or death.

Yet to me, when off duty, London offered a well-heeled idleness, even on £2 5s od a week. After paying for my lodgings I had £1 to spend, which could be broken up in a hundred ways. A tot of whisky cost sixpence, a pint of beer fourpence-halfpenny, cigarettes were elevenpence for twenty. The best seats in the cinema cost ninepence to a shilling, or I could climb to the gallery for threepence. Then there were fairs and music halls, Russian ballet at the Alhambra, Queen's Hall concerts – seldom more than a shilling. Suits made to measure for fifty bob, sixpenny dances, ninepenny suppers – life may have been no cheaper, considering what I was earning, but it seemed so, and I paid no taxes.

It was a time of rootless enjoyment, and also luxurious melancholy which I took care to spin out and nourish. Walking almost everywhere, and most often alone, I studied my shadow, my face in the windows, acknowledging the thrust of London and what it demanded of me – fame and fortune at the very least. This was what I was here for, and what they expected back home. Yet my head was idle and empty.

So I did what I could, short of coming to grips; staring at the river, or playing billiards, and waiting. Writing, destroying, confident of time, wandering the heath, not particularly troubled; or picking up servant girls from the last great houses, gnawing at the chicken-wings they brought me, lying taut among the bushes in the broken lamplight and fancying myself with grander loves.

But mostly I wandered, seeking the spacious exhaustion of brooding energies going to waste. Sometimes, on a day off, I'd walk into the City, along the Embankment and up the Strand, pausing at the Victorian chop-houses to sniff the red sides of beef hanging on hooks in the steaming windows. To me such food was like a mountain of Sundays, or the hot gravied kiss of Mammon, strictly reserved for plump brokers and bankers – it never occurred to me that *I* might eat it.

The City itself, with its courtyards and passages, was familiar, like odd corners of Stroud – faded brass plates nailed to flaking doorways, ancient messengers in mould-green coats, tottering porters carrying coal to stuffy clerk-filled attics, an air of wet biscuits and crumbling parchment. But hooded, cramped, and slyly unrecognizable as the counting-house of the treasuries of the world. And not at all what I expected. It made me uneasy. I always expected to run into my father.

After these trips to the City I'd try a change of style, and turn back into Charing Cross Road, then round off the evening in a Soho café smoking coal-black Mexican cigars. Here, darkly international in my crumpled raincoat, and surrounded by soft-tongued Greeks, I'd open the *Heraldo de Madrid*, which I couldn't read, and order Turkish coffee, which I couldn't drink ...

Half my time, of course, was spent on the buildings, submerged by its mindless, invigorating routine. For almost a year, every weekday morning, I put on my lime-caked clothes, walked up Putney Hill, left my lunch with the tea-boy, and climbed into the windswept scaffolding. I was one of a gang of wheelbarrow-pushers, supplying newly-mixed cement for the floors, rhythmically shuttling to and fro across the springing duckboards and slowly rising as the buildings grew.

For eleven hard months, on the site of that elegant mansion, we raised three unbeautiful blocks of flats – squat, complacent, with mean leaded windows, bogus balconies, and imitation baronials. They were the only things I ever had a hand in building, and I still think of them with some affection, and return there occasionally, even today, to stare amazed at their cramped pretensions.

As builders' labourers, we were the villains of industry and came at the bottom of the hierarchy of the workers. Unskilled, insecure, poorly paid, often dangerous, the job recruited what it could get; and many of my mates were the kind of city-bred dwarf who must have been the result of centuries of thin blood and compression. The type is rarer now, but can still be seen sometimes, perhaps in a Battersea or Wandsworth pub, crouching chin to table with a diminutive wife, feet barely touching the floor. In my day such men were the millstones of labour, ground small by its wasting demands. Yet they were tough, uncomplaining, almost fatalistic, and ageless in look and manner. Physically cramped and hard, with squashed-up limbs, crop-headed and muffler-choked, they spat Cockney from mouths like ruined quarries, and were the natural users of rhyming slang.

This slang seemed still to be the underworld *argot*, a secretive and evasive language, and had not, at that time, been self-consciously elevated into a saloon-bar affectation. When slang was not used, my mates seemed to suffer a curious inhibition, a reluctance to name people and things. ''Ere, what's-yer-name, mate. Chuck us over that what-d'ya-call-it, will yer? Got to make a what's-it fer this thingummy-jig.' I don't think it was laziness or lack of vocabulary, but rather an instinctive concealment which giving names might betray.

At least half of us, certainly, had been recruited from the underworld, apparently a normal practice of the times – we had old lags and con-men temporarily defeated by crime, skilled cracksmen lying low between jobs, and others who had confessed, under pressure, to a wish to reform and seemed to be required to push barrows to prove it. I found myself working with men straight from the Moor, with its gangrenous pallor still on them, and who moved with that head-down shuffle, passive and blind, as though their world was still a walled-in circle. Most of them were natives of Wandsworth and Fulham, reticent but nostalgic men, who would sometimes loosen up with tales of crime and punishment as though ruminating about the war.

In my gang, I remember, we had a little of everything : safe-breakers, cat-men, dopers, a forger ruined by rheumatism, a bigamist past his prime, and a specialist who picked locks with his celluloid shirt collar. On the fringe there was also a sad little clerk who'd served time for raping his daughter, and who no one forgave but condemned to the perpetual torment of sadistic practical jokes. But it was clear that crime had fattened none of them; they were shrivelled by years of attrition, by the staleness of poverty, doubt and suspicion, and by the diminishing returns of jail.

Yet on the whole there was a natural comradeship; there were no cliques and no self-pity. We were in this together and parcelled the job among us, sharing its profit and loss. We covered up for each other if one of our members was ill, or when the foreman was looking for blood. When it rained, we hid, and played pitch-and-toss in the cellars; when fine, we worked by turns, spinning out illusionary jobs in a mime of activity so that no one should be thought redundant. During the lunch-hour we gathered in an old tin shed, ate our scrappy grub off our knees, rolled cigarettes for each other, worked up a fug, and gambled at crown-and-anchor. Gambling was religion, our wages were mortgaged, and piles of notes changed hands, but though some of us flourished, honour was strictly observed, and it was doubtful if anyone cheated. The old lags particularly were the guardians of honour, implacable as Indian chiefs, their black teeth clamped round their tiny pipes, merciless to any back-sliding.

Off the job, walking home, we appeared to be natural targets for old ladies and local policemen. The police always treated us with truculent aggression : the old ladies gave us pennies and crusts. It may have been an instinctive reaction to our caps and mufflers, a hangover from the pages of *Punch*. Anyway, we accepted it, both the kicks and the charity, as part of the traditional perks of our trade. Certainly we were habitual pilferers – though on a job like ours there was little of value that was portable. I, myself, got the habit of carrying off little bits of copper tubing, which I hid down the legs of my trousers. They were smooth, well-turned, and prettily burnished; but I never knew what to do with them.

On the job, as I said, we labourers were the goons, the untouchable fetchers and carriers. Between us and the craftsmen there existed a gulf of caste almost as extreme as anything in India. The bricklayers, carpenters, plasterers and plumbers treated us with the casual contempt of Brahmins, and even at lunchtime they sat by themselves, rigidly wrapped in their status skills. Consequently we hardened ourselves into a compact little group, even more exclusive and cagey than theirs. The use of solidarity was the only skill we had, and I think we would have slain for each other.

There were two exceptions however, two lonely outsiders who, though labourers, we never admitted. One was the middle-aged rapist, our haltered scapegoat, who we reserved for special torment. The other was the old head-gardener, whose garden had disappeared with the house, but who had been allowed to stay on by sufferance, and who was now ending his life tipping barrows of cement over the roots of his ruined roses.

Then in early spring, with the flats half-finished, something happened which threw us all together; something ordinary in itself, but for me an occasion which had much of the punitive, rasping air of the Thirties.

It began one morning with the discovery that some non-union men had been smuggled on to the job by the manager – provocation enough to lower for a moment, at least, the sacred barriers between the trades. Someone sounded the alarm by beating on an iron triangle, and everyone immediately stopped work. Cement mixers coughed and came to a halt; the men swarmed off the rooftops and scrambled down the scaffolding as though abandoning a stricken battleship.

We massed in the open outside the manager's office, our

tempers suddenly transformed – over five hundred men huddled in the raw cold wind, waiting for our ranks to throw up a
leader. At first we were lost; sporadic meetings broke out,
voices shouted against each other. 'Brothers! – Comrades! –
We got to stand solid on this – Chuck 'em out – Put our demands to the bosses.' The loaded phrases touched off little bush-
fires of anger which flickered across the crowd, then died.
Finally the manager sent a message ordering us to return to
work. He'd discuss nothing. We could take it or leave it.

Just then a tall stoop-backed labourer pushed his way to the
front and climbed up on to a pile of timber, and as soon as he
turned to address us we knew that he'd do, and that the
vacuum was filled.

This man was later to become one of the legends of the
Thirties, part of its myth of class struggle and protest – a lean
powerful figure with dangling arms, big fists, and a square
bitter face. His face, in fact, was almost the perfect prototype
of the worker-hero of early Soviet posters – proud, passionate,
merciless, and fanatic, yet deeply scarred by hardship. He was
still in his twenties but already had a history, he'd been jailed
after a naval mutiny, and now as he towered above us, his
voice mangled and eloquent, his finger stabbing the cold spring
air, he stood enlarged on a screen that seemed giant-sized, a
figure straight out of *Potemkin*.

He spoke briefly, with savage almost contemptuous dignity,
and the other gabblers round the ground fell silent. With a few
iron words he raised the level of our grievance to the heights of
cosmic revolution. We had been vague and wavering; now we
had no doubts. We voted for immediate strike.

The manager had been listening at the door of his office,
smirking, and playing with his trilby. When he heard our de-
cision he went pink with rage and began to bounce up and
down like a baby.

'Outside!' he screamed. 'Everyone out this instant! Outside –
or I'll have you arrested for trespassing!'

We filed through the gates and sat down on the Heath, five
hundred men in the rain, and watched as the gates were locked
behind us, and a little later, the police arrived. The half-finished

buildings stood wet and empty, with a look of sudden death. An hour ago we'd been in there, swarming all over them, now a row of black-caped cops stood between us. Such a narrow gap between consent and dispute. We were outlaws now all right. When we approached the police, expecting a bit of traditional banter, they seemed just as livid as the manager.

The strike lasted two weeks – a fortnight of back-street agitation during which I tasted the first sweet whiff of revolution. Without work or status, we lived an underground existence, cut off from the rule of law, meeting in cafés and basements, drawing up manifestoes, planning demonstrations, painting placards and posters. In this hazy ghetto of ideological struggle it was easy to lose our dimensions, and the immediate aims of the strike became so blurred that we felt ready to take on the world. It was then, for the first time, that I experienced hallucinations of communism, naïve and innocent as water, a physical sensation rather than an intellectual one, like a weekend at a holiday camp. I began to see visions of the day when the workers would triumph, and we would be running with flags through the streets, the bosses in flight, the temples of privilege falling, other workers waiting to join us, to inherit a scrubbed new world of open-necked shirts, bare arms flexed in common labour, with perhaps a hint of free love shared with our prettier comrades, and communal nurseries crammed with our gold-haired offspring.

Then, suddenly, the strike was over, closed by a grudging agreement, and we were back at work again; back at dodging the foreman and gambling in corners, unchanged except for two weeks' hunger.

Now I'd been nearly a year in London, and had little to show for it except calloused hands and one printed poem. Life at Mrs Flynn's was a little odder, but as comfortable as ever, and she had a new boy-friend who increased the amenities.

One of these was Clara, an orphan from Battersea, who he'd hired to help with the cleaning – a thin rakey child of about fifteen who never spoke when grown-ups were around. She would gossip and play with little Patsy, but otherwise she worked in silence, a fugitive figure of fits and starts in constant agony of being noticed. I never knew Clara, but she seemed to have her private consolations, and also ways of making herself known. Sometimes I'd come home at night and turn on the switch in my room to find that she'd removed all the electric light bulbs. 'Is that you, Laurie?' shrieked Mrs Flynn from the basement. 'Don't worry, the poor love can't 'elp it.' Then I'd find the electric bulbs in my bed, arranged like a nest of eggs, with one of her shoes or perhaps an old doll of Patsy's.

Patsy herself had grown more torrid with the months and had begun to practise with paint and lipstick, appearing suddenly at my door with scarified mouth and cheeks like Shakespeare's apparition of a bloody child. Shadowy Beth continued to pamper me, and to feed me on large late suppers, hovering with a tight tired smile to see that I had all I wanted, or to explain that Patsy was growing up. Mrs Flynn, more valiantly blonde then ever, and temporarily airborne by social success, regularly returned half my rent with gifts of beer and tobacco, and kept insisting that no one get married. In fact I was pampered by all of them, wrapped in a deep cushioned groove and guarded like some exotic lemur. There seemed to be no good reason why I shouldn't make a life of it here, except that I didn't want to end up in the attic, like Mr Willow.

By early summer the flats were almost completed, and I knew I would soon be out of a job. There was no prospect of another, but I wasn't worried; I never felt so beefily strong in my life. I remember standing one morning on the windy rooftop, and looking round at the racing sky, and suddenly realizing that once the job was finished I could go anywhere I liked in the world.

There was nothing to stop me, I would be penniless, free, and could just pack up and walk away. I was a young man whose time coincided with the last years of peace, and so was perhaps luckier than any generation since. Europe at least was wide open, a place of casual frontiers, few questions and almost no travellers.

So where should I go? It was just a question of getting there

– France? Italy? Greece? I knew nothing at all about any of them, they were just names with vaguely operatic flavours. I knew no languages either, so felt I could arrive new-born wherever I chose to go. Then I remembered that somewhere or other I'd picked up a phrase in Spanish for 'Will you please give me a glass of water?' and it was probably this rudimentary bit of lifeline that finally made up my mind. I decided I'd go to Spain.

So as soon as I was sacked from the buildings, at the beginning of June, I bought a one-way ticket to Vigo. I remember it cost £4, which left me with a handful of shillings to see me safely into Spain. I didn't bother to wonder what would happen then, for already I saw myself there, brown as an apostle, walking the white dust roads through the orange groves.

The ship wasn't due to sail for a couple of weeks, so I spent my last days in London with a girl called Nell, who I'd found in a cinema. She came from Balham, and we used to meet on the Heath and then sometimes go to my room. She was soft and nervous, creamily pretty, buxom, yet plaintively chaste. Intoxicated by idleness – she was out of work too – and by the aura of incipient farewell, she used to lie in my arms in the summer dusk, struggling to save us both from sin. She wore the loose peasant blouse that was the fashion of the day, a panting bundle of creviced cotton, and as our time grew shorter she grew larger and softer as though all her frontiers were melting away. Then our last night came: 'Perhaps you could tie my hands. Then I couldn't say nothing, could I?' Finally: 'Take me with you. I wouldn't be any trouble.' I felt light-headed, detached, and heartless. 'Take me with you' was something I was also hearing from other girls, who seemed not to have noticed me till now. For the first time I was learning how much easier it was to leave than to stay behind and love.

The morning came for departure, and the children helped me pack and Mike gave me his pocket jack-knife. Beth had gone off to work, leaving me a note of farewell, and Mrs Flynn was still asleep. Patsy walked half-way to the station with me, and we stopped on Putney Bridge. It was a fine chill morning, with a light mist on the river and the tide running fast to the sea.

Patsy stood on tip-toe and grabbed hold of my ear and pulled it down to her paint-smeared mouth. 'Take me with you,' she said, then gave a quick snort of laughter, waved good-bye, and ran back home.

# 3. Into Spain

It was early and still almost dark when our ship reached the harbour, and when out of the unconscious rocking of sea and sleep I was simultaneously woken and hooked to the coast of Spain by the rattling anchor going over the side.

Lying safe in the old ship's blousy care, I didn't want to move at first. I'd enjoyed the two slow days coming down the English Channel and across the Bay of Biscay, smelling the soft Gulf winds blowing in from the Atlantic and feeling the deep easy roll of the ship. But this was Vigo, the name on my ticket, and as far as its protection would take me. So I lay for a while in the anchored silence and listened to the first faint sounds of Spain – a howling dog, the gasping spasms of a donkey, the thin sharp cry of a cockerel. Then I packed and went up on to the shining deck, and the Spanish sun rose too, and for the first time in my life I saw, looped round the bay, the shape of a foreign city.

I'd known nothing till then but the smoother surfaces of England, and Vigo struck me like an apparition. It seemed to rise from the sea like some rust-corroded wreck, as old and bleached as the rocks around it. There was no smoke or movement among the houses. Everything looked barnacled, rotting, and deathly quiet, as though awaiting the return of the Flood. I landed in a town submerged by wet green sunlight and smelling of the waste of the sea. People lay sleeping in doorways, or sprawled on the ground, like bodies washed up by the tide.

But I was in Spain, and the new life beginning. I had a few shillings in my pocket and no return ticket; I had a knapsack, blanket, spare shirt, and a fiddle, and enough words to ask for a glass of water. So the chill of dawn left me and I began to feel better. The drowned men rose from the pavements and stretched their arms, lit cigarettes, and shook the night from their clothes. Bootblacks appeared, banging their brushes together, and strange vivid girls went down the streets, with hair like coils of dripping tar and large mouths, red and savage.

Still a little off balance I looked about me, saw obscure dark eyes and incomprehensible faces, crumbling walls scribbled with mysterious graffiti, an armed policeman sitting on the Town Hall steps, and a photograph of Marx in a barber's window. Nothing I knew was here, and perhaps there was a moment of panic – anyway I suddenly felt the urge to get moving. So I cut the last cord and changed my shillings for pesetas, bought some bread and fruit, left the seaport behind me and headed straight for the open country.

I spent the rest of the day climbing a steep terraced valley, then camped for the night on a craggy hilltop. Some primitive instinct had forced me to leave the road and climb to this rocky tower, which commanded an eagle's view of the distant harbour and all the hills and lagoons around it. Here, sitting on a stone, about six miles inland, I could look out in all directions, see where I was in the landscape, where I'd been that day, and much of the country still to come. Wild and silent, like a picture of western Ireland, it rolled rhythmically and desolately away, and faced with its alien magnificence I felt a last pang of homesickness, and the first twinge of uneasy excitement.

The Galician night came quickly, the hills turned purple and the valleys flooded with heavy shadow. The jagged coastline below, now dark and glittering, looked like sweepings of broken glass. Vigo was cold and dim, an unlighted ruin, already smothered in the dead blue dusk. Only the sky and the ocean stayed alive, running with immense streams of flame. Then as the sun went down it seemed to drag the whole sky with it like the shreds of a burning curtain, leaving rags of bright water that went on smoking and smouldering along the estuaries and around the many islands. I saw the small white ship, my last link with home, flare like a taper and die away in the darkness; then I was alone at last, sitting on a hilltop, my teeth chattering as the night wind rose.

I found a rough little hollow out of the wind, a miniature crater among the rocks, ate some bread and dates, unrolled the blanket and wrapped myself inside it. I laid the fiddle beside me, used the knapsack as a pillow, and stretched out on the bed of stones; then folded my hands, hooked my little fingers together, shut my eyes and prepared to sleep.

But I slept little that night: I was attacked by wild dogs – or they may have been Galician wolves. They came slinking and snarling along the ridge of my crater, hackles bristling against the moon, and only by shouting, throwing stones, and flashing my torch in their eyes was I able to keep them at bay. Not till early dawn did they finally leave me and run yelping away down the hillside, when I fell at last into a nightmare doze, feeling their hot yellow teeth in my bones.

When I awoke next morning it was already light, and voices were screaming at one another in the valley. I looked at my watch and it was six o'clock, and I was heavily drenched in dew. I wriggled out of the blanket, crawled on to the ridge and lay in the rising sun, and was met by the resinous smell of drying bushes, peppery herbs, and stones. As I warmed my stiff limbs, I looked down the valley from which the sharp hard cries were coming, and saw a group of old women, as black as charcoal, slapping out sheets along the banks of a stream. Galician peasants, women *and* Spanish, unknown and doubly inscrutable – their thin bent bodies knelt over the water, jerking up and down like drinking hens, and as they worked they shrieked, firing off metallic bursts of speech that bounced off the rocks like bullets.

I lay on my belly, the warm earth against me, and forgot the cold dew and the wolves of the night. I felt it was for this I had come; to wake at dawn on a hillside and look out on a world for which I had no words, to start at the beginning, speechless and without plan, in a place that still had no memories for me.

For as I woke that second morning, with the whole of Spain to walk through, I was in a country of which I knew nothing. The names of Velasquez, Goya, El Greco, Lope de Vega, Juan de la Cruz were unknown to me; I'd never heard of the Cordovan Moors or the Catholic kings; nor of the Alhambra or the Escorial; or that Trafalgar was a Spanish Cape, Gibraltar a Spanish rock, or that it was from here that Columbus had sailed for America. My small country school, always generous with its information as to the exports of Queensland and the fate of Jenkins's ear, had provided me with nothing more tangible or useful about Spain than that Seville had a barber, and Barcelona, nuts.

But I was innocent then of my ignorance, and so untroubled by it. My clothes steamed and dried as the sun grew stronger. The distant sea shone white, a clean morning freshness after last night's smoky fires. The rising hills before me went stepping away inland, fiercely shaped under the great blue sky. I nibbled some bread and fruit, rolled my things in a bundle, and washed my head and feet in a spring. Then shouldering my burden, and still avoiding the road, I took a track south-east for Zamora.

For three or four days I followed the track through the hills, but saw only occasional signs of life – sometimes a shepherd's hut, or a distant man walking, or a solitary boy with a flock of goats; otherwise no sound or movement except the eagles overhead and the springs gushing out of the rocks. The track climbed higher into the clear cold air, and I just followed it, hoping to keep direction. When twilight came, I curled up where I was, too exhausted to mind the cold. One night I took shelter in a ruined castle which I found piled on top of a crag – a gaunt roofless fortress tufted with the nests of ravens and scattered with abandoned fires. The skeleton of a sheep stood propped in one corner, picked clean, like a wicker basket; and drawings of women and horses were scratched round the walls. An obvious refuge, I thought, for bandits. But I slept well enough in the tottering place, in spite of its audible darkness, the rustling in the walls, the squeaks and twitters, and the sighing of the mountain wind.

Otherwise all I remember of those first days from Vigo is a deliriously sharpening hunger, an appetite so keen it seemed almost a pity to satisfy it, so voluptuous it was.

By the second day I'd finished my bread and dates, but I found a few wild grapes and ate them green, and also the remains of a patch of beans.

Then I remember coming out of a gorge one early evening and seeing my first real village. I remember it well, because it was like all Spain, and it was also my first encounter. It stood on a bare brown rock in the sinking sun – a pile of squat houses like cubes of pink sugar. In the centre rose a tower from which a great black bell sent out cracked jerking gusts of vibration. I'd had enough of the hills and lying around in wet bracken, and now I smelt fires and a sweet tang of cooking. I climbed the steep road into the village, and black-robed women, standing in doorways, made soft exclamations as I went by.

In the village square I came on a great studded door bearing the sign: 'Posada de Nuestra Señora.' I pushed the door open and entered a whitewashed courtyard hanging with geraniums and crowded with mules and asses. There was bedlam in the courtyard – mules stamping, asses braying, chickens cackling, and children fighting. A fat old crone, crouching by the fire in the corner, was stirring soup in a large black cauldron, and as she seemed to be in charge I went up to her and made a sign for food. Without a word she lifted a ladleful of the soup and held it up to my mouth. I tasted and choked; it was hot, strong, and acrid with smoke and herbs. The old lady peered at me sharply through the fumes of the fire. She was bent, leather-skinned, bearded and fanged, and looked like a watchful moose. I wiped my burnt mouth, nodded my head, and said 'Good' in clear loud English. She took a long pull herself, her moustached lips working, her eyes rolling back in her skull. Then she spat briskly into the fire, turned her head abruptly and roared out in a deep hoarse voice – and a barefooted boy, dressed only in a shirt, came and tugged my sleeve and led me to see the bed-rooms.

Later I was sitting in the courtyard under the swinging light-bulbs, hungrily watching the supper cooking, when the inn-keeper came out, a towel round his waist, and began to scrub his young son in the horse-trough. The infant screamed, the old crone roared, the father shouted, sang, and lathered. Then sud-denly, as by a whim, he shoved the child under the water and left him to see what he'd do. The screams were cut off as though by a knife, while the old woman and the father watched him. In a fierce choking silence the child fought the water, kicking and struggling like a small brown frog, eyes open, mouth working, his whole body grappling with the sudden inexplicable threat of death. He was about one year old, but for a moment seemed ageless, facing terror alone and dumb. Then just as he was about to give in, the woman picked up a bucket and threw it at the father's head, and at that he snatched up the child, tossed him in the air, smothered him with kisses, and carried him away.

Supper was laid at last on the long wooden table set out under the open sky. When it was ready the innkeeper, with a sweep of his arm, invited me to join them. Carters and drovers gathered quickly round the table, and a girl dealt out loaves to each of us, and we ate the stew from a common dish, scooping it up with our bread. The old woman sat beside me and roared at me continuously, pinching my legs and thumping me in the belly and urging me on to eat.

Half-way through supper we were joined by two shifty-eyed men who came in carrying a new-skinned lamb. They looked starved, desperate, and poor as dogs, and their shirts hung in rags from their shoulders. They approached us in silence and nobody greeted them, nor did they seem to expect it. They dropped the bleeding lamb at the far end of the table, threw themselves down, and called for wine. Then they began to tear at the carcass, cramming the meat in their mouths and darting fugitive looks over their shoulders. Their movements had all the sharp snapping nervousness of beasts at a kill, crouching low and cracking the bones with their teeth. When a girl had brought them their wine, they were left to themselves – their meal was their own secret business.

At our end of the table, supper was prolonged and noisy, and I didn't know whether it was night or morning. By now I was gorged with stew and warmed to idiocy by wine; I was the stranger, but I felt at home. In each face around me I seemed to recognize characters from my own village : the carters, inn-keepers, the dust-covered farmboys, grandmothers, and girls, they were all here. I felt like a child crawling on the edge of some rousing family life which I had yet to grow to understand. And I think they felt it too, for they treated me like a child – grinning, shouting, acting dumb-shows to please me, and smoothing my way with continual tit-bits and indulgencies.

At last supper was over. The women swept the dishes away, and the carters curled up on the ground to sleep. The two outcasts lay snoring across their end of the table, their faces buried in a debris of bones. I rose from my chair and stumbled away to my room, where I found six beds, full of men and fleas. Fowls were roosting in the rafters, and an old man lay fully clothed on the floor, fast asleep, with a goat tethered to his ankle. The room was stifling, but the straw bed was soft. And there I slept, my head roaring with Spain.

That was just one night, an early one on my journey, and also my first inn, like many others to come. From then on the days merged into a continuous movement of sun and shadow, hunger and thirst, fatigue and sleep, all fused and welded into one coloured mass by the violent heat of that Spanish summer.

I had come now out of the hills of Galicia, along high bare tracks overhanging the sheltered valleys where thick grass grew and herds of panting sheep gathered at noon by white-pebbled streams. I had skirted the mountains of León, coming through shaded oak-woods and groves of fig and almond, along great shelves of rock where wooden ox-carts laboured and boys in broad hats went leaping up the hillsides pursuing their scattered flocks. I'd come through poor stone villages, full of wind and dust, where mobs of children convoyed me through the streets, and where priests and women quickly crossed themselves when they saw me, and there was nothing to buy except sunflower seeds. And I'd come down at last to the rich plain of the Douro, with its fields of copper earth, its violent outcrops of poppies running in bloodstained bandannas across acres of rasping wheat.

After the green of the hills the light here was lethal; it thumped the head and screwed up the eyes. I was burnt by the sun, and bug-ridden from the inns – but I was also slowly beginning to pick up the language. Listening to people on the road I noticed that their guttural flow had begun to break up and detach into words and phrases: 'good', 'bad', 'bread and wine', 'how much?' 'too much; shame...' So without more inhibition I started talking to everyone, offering anything that came to mind, and many a sombre patriarch jogging towards me on his mule would be met by some stumbling salutation, and would raise a stiff grave hand in defence and greeting, and bid me go with God.

I finally reached Zamora early one Saturday evening, after a blistering day through the wheatfields. The town stood neatly stacked on its rocky hill, a ripple of orange roofs and walls, somewhat decrepit now, but still giving off something of the medieval sternness and isolated watchfulness of its past. Around its rocky site curled the track of the Douro, a leathery arm of wrinkled mud, laced down the middle with a vein of green water in which some half-naked boys were bathing.

Brick-red with road-dust I padded into the square and sat down under a shady plane tree. After the long day's walk my back was sheeted with sweat and my bag was like a load of stones. I slipped it to the ground and sucked in the hot still air; the evening was thunderous and swimming with flies. There was almost no one in the square except a few old women and a man selling mineral water. Seeing my parched condition, he came and gave me a bottle, but refused to take any payment. The pink scented juice tasted like effervescent hair-oil, but it instantly revived me.

As I sat there, scratching, and wondering where I would spend the night, I suddenly heard the sound of music coming from a nearby street – not the Spanish kind, but waltzy gusts of Strauss played on accordion, flute, and fiddle. Curious, I went off to have a look, and found three blond young men bashing out a back-street concert in the midst of a crowd of wide-mouthed children. Men had halted their mules, women stood listening in doorways or hung from balconies overhead. The syrupy beer-hall strains of 'Vienna Woods' swept incongruously round the Spanish houses, but the boys were doing well – pennies tumbled from windows or were tossed over the heads of the children, to be caught with a flourish in the fiddler's hat with heavily accented thanks.

It was a significant moment, and I was cheered by the sight, as this was how I, too, hoped to live. It seemed that I'd come to the right country, poor as it was; the pennies were few, but they were generously given. And music was clearly welcome in this Spanish street, the faces softened with pleasure as they listened.

When they'd finished their playing, the boys spotted me in the crowd, nodded gaily, and addressed me in German. I explained where I came from, which wasn't what they expected, then we sat on the pavement and chattered in broken English. They were about my own age, and displayed a high-strung energy, busy eyes, and a kind of canine sharpness. They were from Hamburg, they said, and had been in Spain two years, had circled it twice and were planning to circle it again.

They called themselves students, and said there were a large number in the country, playing instruments and living rough – partly for fun, and partly to get out of Germany: I was the first 'student' they'd met from England. Meanwhile, they introduced themselves – Artur, Rudi, and Heinrich – and invited me to spend the evening with them.

After I, in turn, had given them an account of myself, and they had examined my clothes and blisters, they took me to a shop to buy some cool light sandals, and picked out a beggar on whom to bestow my boots. Then we went to a bar to count out the concert money and drink some of the thin warm, local beer. Artur was full of advice, and seemed to know Zamora well. 'Is beaudival place, but poor as church rats. Tomorrow is going away.'

Germans, of course, had been the folk-devils of my childhood, the bogies of all our games. These ragged young lads, noisily sucking their beer, were the first real Germans I'd ever met. Artur was their leader, and played the violin. He was tall, curly with a long mobile throat, sunken cheeks, and feverish blue eyes. He talked with a jerking vitality that seemed close to hysteria, face sweating, eyes rolling, his speech often broken into by jagged rasps of consumptive coughing. Rudi was young and quieter, and sat stroking his accordion and humming tunes through his fat red lips. Heinrich, the flautist, was as agreeable as a dog, and sat panting at Artur's feet – strung-up, on edge, and watching him intently, ready for any game or change of humour. He was a clown, if needed, and poured Artur's beer, and carried his supply of paper handkerchiefs.

'Now for the danze!' cried Artur. Night had fallen already, and the boys had a job at the local dance-hall. 'Are making the music,' he said. 'Ya, one – two – three! Are drinking the beer and coming many girls. Afterwards good essen, and you can be sleeping in our room, very cheap, you can imagine.'

So we took my things to the lodging house, then headed for the dance-hall down by the river. The town was palely lit by naked yellow bulbs which gave an impression of curried moonlight. As we went down the narrow cobble-stepped streets, Rudi struck up on his accordion, playing wild banshee scales designed to advertise the dance and to summon the youth of the town. He succeeded too : sleeping pigeons took off, dogs barked, and windows flew open, and very soon we had a procession of well-brushed customers hurrying along behind us.

'Look, I say!' cried Artur excitedly, gripping my arm and sawing the air with it. 'See are coming many boys and girls. You shall make danze with them all, nothing forbidden, you understand.'

The dance-hall was a kind of brokendown warehouse propped up on the river bank, just a bare wooden shack dressed with a few old chairs and some primitive decorations. When you stepped on the floorboards they went off like fireworks, raising little puffballs of peppery dust, and there were holes in the roof through which you could see the stars whenever the dust allowed it. Around the walls hung pictures of half-naked women, clenching roses in desperate teeth, and wearing loose cardboard flaps round their ample loins which the curious could raise to reveal slogans for beer. There was also an improvised bar, some strings of paper carnations, and a platform draped with the Spanish flag.

As they poured into the room, the dancers immediately segregated themselves, girls down one side, boys down the other. Considerably quieter now than they had been in the street, the boys looked pale and anxious, rubbing their hands on their knees, tapping their neat little feet, and gazing at the girls with potent gloom. The girls were far more self-possessed, knowing their worth on such occasions, settling plump in their chairs like bags of sweets, stickily scented and tied with ribbons.

The band tuned up noisily, then Artur swayed to his feet and announced a pasodoble. The barriers fell at once, and the dancing began and the noise it made was soon as loud as the band. The boys stamped like bulls, the girls twirled and shuffled, dust rose, and the floorboards jumped. Caught face to face, away from their neutral corners, the dancers grappled in passionate strife – but as soon as the music ended, the girls turned chastely away, leaving the boys flatfooted.

For an hour or so I sat on the platform with the band

sharing their gifts of bottled beer. It was warm, scummy, and rather sour, but it had a lively effect on Artur. Soon his fiddle was soaring above the sounds of the flute, departing on a life of its own, playing thin little tunes of Bavarian extraction which only he and I could hear. For a while, eyes closed, he was no longer with us, he was away in the forest snows.

Suddenly he looked at me.

'Is not good time?' he shouted. 'But why is not danzing, yah?' He looked round the room, spotted an unused girl, and called her over to join me.

What with my blistered feet, and the beer in my head, it was as much as I could do to stand up. But the girl took charge – she just wrapped her damp arms round me, propped me snugly erect with her bosom, and away we went over the flapping floorboards as though skating on Venetian blinds. This stumbling movement, together with the unexpected nearness of the girl, did nothing to lessen my feeling of drunkenness. Several times I would have fallen, but the girl was like scaffolding, like a straight-jacket of cushioned bones. Helpless, half-crippled, half-anaesthetized by her scent, I scuffled after her, praying for the end. She was tough and beautiful, but I could think of nothing to say to her – except Help, I feel sick and hungry. Finally the waltz was over, and the girl led me back to my chair and seated me carefully in it. As she left me she drew her finger down the length of my body as though sealing an envelope.

It was long after midnight before the dancers went home, fading crushed and bruised into the darkness. Suddenly there was no one in the hall but the Germans and myself, and the waiters picking up empty bottles. The floor was littered with paper carnations, and white dust covered everything like frost.

'Eating now,' croaked Artur. He leant exhausted against the wall, bathed in sweat, trembling like a race-horse. Heinrich took off his jacket and threw it round Artur's shoulders, and we went out into the starlit street. As soon as the cold air met us, Artur's coughing began, and we followed it like a death-knell up through the silent town to the café where supper was waiting.

Artur had fixed it: roast kid and beans – a miracle at this hour of the morning. We slumped round the table, weary and famished, and an old woman brought us some wine. Then we gorged ourselves, using our fingers and winking at one another. The meat had a flavour and tenderness I shall never forget, it came off the bone like petals from a rose.

It seemed that nothing could quieten Artur now. He giggled, whinnied, and coughed out his lungs; his eyes rolled and his lips were flecked. But gradually the food and the wine composed and drowsed him. Heinrich held him by the shoulders and cradled his head. Rudi sang softly at the other end of the table. It was nearly dawn, but no one wished to move. We felt pitiful and sentimental.

We carried Artur like a corpse to the room upstairs, which had four beds, but no light or windows. Someone found a candle, and we lay Artur down, took off his boots, and Heinrich wiped his forehead. Nobody spoke any more, or even whispered; we went to our beds and Rudi blew out the candle. I lay sleepless for a while in the death-room darkness, my first and last night in Zamora, listening to the choking rattle of Artur's breath, and the sound of Heinrich weeping.

# 4. Zamora—Toro

It was a short sleep and a brutal waking, roused by Artur's reluctant resurrection, while he sat swaying on his bed raked by paroxysms of coughing, his face the colour of crumpled pewter.

We revived him slowly in the tavern below, and then decided that it was time for us to leave. One night of music and dance had emptied the coffers of the city so far as the German boys were concerned. 'Is poor as church rats,' repeated Artur painfully. 'Is better going, you can imagine.'

At midday we packed and walked out of the town and paused for a moment at a fork in the road – one way leading north to León and Oviedo, and the other eastward to Valladolid. This was where we parted. The boys were going to León, where they would join some other 'students', while I'd chosen Valladolid, not because I knew anything about it, but because I liked the sound of its syllables.

At the waste edge of Zamora, a dismal litter of dust with donkeys grazing among bones and bottles, the boys formally shook my hand. The bare tight-laced city rose moodily behind us, its twelfth-century cathedral looking bleached like driftwood.

'Good-bye,' spluttered Artur. 'We see you again and again.' We went our different ways.

Almost immediately I regretted the cool alleys of the town, the scrubbed taverns and frothy fruit-drinks. By the afternoon I was out in the plain, in an electric haze of heat, walking a white dust road as straight as a canal, banked by shimmering wheat and poppies. For mile after mile I saw neither man nor beast; the world seemed to be burnt out, drained and dead; and the blinding white road, narrowing away to the horizon, began to fill me with curious illusions. I felt I was treading the rim of a burning wheel, kicking it behind me step by step, feet scorched and blistered, yet not advancing an inch, pinned for ever at this sweltering spot. For hours, it seemed, I had the same poppy beside me, the same cluster of brittle wheat, the same goldleaf lizard flickering around my toes, the same ant-hill under the bank. The thick silent dust, lifted by shudders of heat rather than by the presence of any wind, crept into my sandals and between my toes, stuck like rime to my lips and eyelashes, and dropped into the breathless cups of the roadside poppies to fill them with a cool white mirage of snow. All around me was silence, deep and dazed, except for the gritty rustle of the wheat. I walked head down, not daring to look at the sky, which by now seemed to be one huge sun.

That Zamoran wheat-plain was my first taste of Spanish heat – the brass-taloned lion which licks the afternoon ground ready to consume anyone not wise enough to take cover. Exposed to its rasping tongue, I learnt soon enough one of the obvious truths of summer, that no man, beast, or bird – and indeed very few insects – moved much at that time of the day.

About five o'clock, after some four hours on the road, I at last saw a break in the landscape – a red clay village, dry as the earth around it and compact as a termite's nest. I have forgotten its name, and can find nothing marked there on the map, but it occurred at just the right moment.

I stumbled out of the wheatfield on to this evening village to find it in the drowsy grip of harvest. The sun was low already and a coppery dust filled the air, slashed by smouldering shafts of light. In a cleared space by the roadside the menfolk were threshing, driving little sleigh-carts over the scattered sheaves, each drawn by a mule wearing garlands of leaves to keep off the sleepy flies. Women and girls, in broad hats and veils, looking as mysterious as Minoan dancers, stood in graceful circles winnowing the grain in the wind, tossing and catching it in drifts of gold. Rhythmically working at their various jobs, and gilded from head to foot with chaff, the villagers clustered together round the threshing floor like a swarm of summer-laden bees.

Some of them shouted a greeting as I approached, while the women paused to line up and stare; then children ran from the alleys and encircled me and ushered me noisily into the village.

'Look at the foreigner!' they cried, as though they had made me up. 'Look at the rubio who's come today.' They aped my walk, and grinned and beckoned, and finally led me to the village inn.

It was much like the others, with a great oak door. The children pushed it open and stood courteously aside. Nodding and beaming, with brilliant smiles of reassurance, they gestured for me to go in.

So I went inside, and found the usual spacious barn hanging with freshly watered flowers. A few low chairs stood around the walls, and there was a table and tiled stove in the corner. All was cool and bare. Chickens pecked at the floor and swallows flashed from the high arched ceiling.

A middle-aged woman sat just inside the door, stitching at a piece of lace. She was fleshy, but handsome, with the strong brooding eyes and confident mouth of the matriarch. The children crowded the doorway, watching me expectantly as though I was a firework just about to go off, while the small ones at the back jumped up and down in order to get a better view. 'Doña Maria!' they shouted. 'We have brought you a Frenchman. Doña Maria, look at him!'

The woman put down her sewing and thanked them politely, then let out a screech that sent them scattering up the street. After which she considered me for a moment over the top of her steel-rimmed spectacles, then said: 'Rest, and I'll get you some food.'

I slumped down at the table and lay with my head in my arms, listening voluptuously to the woman's movements: the rattle of the pan on the fire, the crack of an eggshell, the hiss of frying oil. Sweat dripped from my hair and ran over my hands, and my head was swimming with heat, with throbbing visions of the white dust road and the brassy glare of the fields.

Presently the woman pushed some fried eggs before me, and poured me a glass of purple wine. Then she returned to her sewing and was joined by a girl, and together they sat and watched me. In that great bare room under the diving swallows, I ate the honoured meal of the stranger, while the women murmured together in low furred voices, their needles darting like silver fish.

At dusk an old man came in from threshing, shaking the chaff from his hair. He poured himself some wine and sat down at the table.

'What have we?' he asked the woman.

She dropped her hands in her lap, and looked at me again, sharply but protectively.

'Ah,' she said. 'He comes from somewhere away. A poor devil who is walking the world.'

The man filled up my glass and jerked his thumb to his mouth. 'Drink, and may it give you strength.'

'You want to sleep here tonight?' asked Doña Maria after a while.

'How much?'

'For a straw sack – two pennies.'

'Good,' I said. 'Then I will sleep with you.'

'No – you will sleep on the sack.'

The old man wheezed, the girl covered her face, and the woman piled her sewing on top of her head. Then with a click of her tongue she heaved her bulk from the chair and skipped lightly towards the stove.

Two dusty young men came through the open door, leading a pig and a sheep on a rope. 'My sons,' said the woman. They poured water over their heads, then filled up the trough for the animals. Mother and daughter set the table for supper, while the old man continued to pour me wine. Then with formal excuses and requests for forgiveness, the family began its meal.

The evening now was close and smoky. The lamp was lit, and the great doors shut. I was getting used to this pattern of Spanish life, which could have been that of England two centuries earlier. This house, like so many others I'd seen already, held nothing more than was useful for living – no fuss of furniture and unnecessary decoration – being as self-contained as the Ark. Pots, pans, the chairs and tables, the manger and drinking-trough, all were of wood, stone, or potter's clay, simply shaped and polished like tools. At the end of the day, the doors and windows admitted all the creatures of the family: father, son, daughter, cousin, the donkey, the pig, the hen, even the harvest mouse and the nesting swallow, bedded together at the fall of darkness.

So it was with us in this nameless village; night found us wrapped in this glowing barn, family and stranger gathered round the long bare table to a smell of woodsmoke, food, and animals. Across the whitewashed walls the shadows of man and beast flickered huge like ancestral ghosts, which since the days of the caves have haunted the corners of fantasy, but which the electric light has killed.

We sat close together, the men drinking and smoking, elbows at rest among the empty plates. It was the short drowsy space between work and sleep, with nothing left of the day but gossip. Doña Maria, who was cobbling a piece of tattered harness, dominated the table with her thick warm voice, telling tales which to me were inscrutable, alas, but which to the others seemed vaguely familiar. The old man was a motionless mask in the shadows, though he showed a tooth in an occasional cackle. The sons sat near me, nudging me politely in the ribs and nodding their heads whenever the mother made a joke. The daughter, sitting close to the only lamp, buried her fingers in her sewing and listened, raising her huge Arab eyes every moment or so, to meet my glance of dumb conjecture.

I was half drunk now; in fact I felt like a bonfire, full of dull smoke and hot congestion. My eyes were hopelessly moored to those small neat breasts, rocking sadly to their rise and fall, till she seeemed to be floating before me on waves of breath, naked as a Negress in her tight black dress.

But the brothers surrounded me, and Doña Maria crouched near, watching me with warm but suspicious indulgence. So I sat and swayed in my drowsy conflagration, fitting sentences together in my mind, then producing them slowly, like a string of ill-knotted flags, for the family's polite astonishment.

Suddenly, one of the sons spotted my rolled-up blanket with the violin sticking out of it. 'Música !' he cried, and went and fetched the bundle and laid it gingerly on the table before me.

'Yes, man,' said the mother. 'Come, divert us a little. Touch us a little tune.' The old man woke up, and the daughter put down her sewing, lifted her head, and even smiled.

There was nothing else for it. I sat down on the ground and tore drunkenly into an Irish reel. They listened, open-mouthed, unable to make head or tail of it; I might have been playing a Tibetan prayer-wheel. Then I tried a woozy fandango which I'd picked up in Zamora, and comprehension jerked them to life. The girl stiffened her body, the boys grabbed a handful of spoons and began slapping them across their knees, and the woman leapt to her feet and started stamping the ground, raising great clouds of dust around me. Not to be outdone, the old man left the shadows, struck a posture, and faced the woman. Doña Maria all flesh, he thin as a straw, together they began a dance of merciless contest, while the boys thumped their spoons, the woman shouted 'Ha!' and the hens flew squawking under the table.

It was no longer just a moment of middle-aged horseplay. The old man danced as if his life was at stake. While the woman was suddenly transformed, her great lumpen body becoming a thing of controlled and savage power. Moving with majestic assurance, her head thrown back, her feet pawing the ground like an animal, she stamped and postured round her small hopping husband as if she would tread him into oblivion. The dance was soon over, but while it lasted she was a woman unsheathed and terrible. Then the old man fell back, threw up his hands in defeat, and retired gasping to the safety of the walls.

The woman was left alone, and the mantle fell from her, and she stood like a girl, mopping her face and giggling, deprecating her performance with little hen-like cluckings and surprised shakings of her head.

'This is not for an old woman. My bones ache,' she said.

'Egyptian!' hissed the man from the shadows.

The sons asked me for another tune, and this time they danced together, with linked arms, rather sedate and formal. The daughter came quietly and sat on the floor beside me, watching my fingers as I played. The scent of her nearness swam troublesomely around me with a mixture of pig's lard and sharp clean lavender.

The evening's routine had been broken, and no one seemed eager to sleep. So some further celebration was possible. The girl was asked to sing, and she did as she was told, in a flat unaffected voice. The songs were simple and moving, and probably local; anyway, I've never heard them since. She sang them innocently, without art, taking breath like a child, often in the middle of a word. Staring blankly before her, without movement or expression, she simply went through each one, then stopped – as though she'd really no idea what the songs were about, only that they were using her to be heard.

With the singing over, we sat in silence for a while, hearing only the trembling sound of the lamp. Then the woman grunted and spoke, and the boys got up from the table and fetched the mattresses and laid them down by the wall.

'You sleep there,' said the mother. 'My sons will watch you.' She pulled knowingly at one of her eyelids. 'Come then,' she added, and the girl rose from her knees and followed her quickly to another part of the house, while the husband's crinkled old face simply disappeared from the air, soundlessly, like a snuffed-out candle.

I was ready for sleep, and stretched myself out on the floor while the boys went and bolted the door. Then they came, fully-clothed, and lay down on each side of me, settling their limbs with little grunts.

The boys were up early, at about half past four, coughing and stamping around the barn. The doors were thrown open to let in the cold pink dawn, and the animals were driven out to the fields. I was still heavy with wine and would have liked more sleep, but it was made clear that the day had started, and soon the girl was about with her birch-twig broom sweeping the chickens across my face.

So I got up from the floor and shook the straw from my clothes, and the girl kicked my mattress into the corner. Then she led me out into the yard, showed me how to use the pump, went through the motions of lathering her face, gave me a piece of soap as hard as a stone, and then departed to light the stove.

Breakfast was a wedge of dry bread and a bowl of soup-thick coffee floating with fatty gobs of goat's milk. By the time I'd swallowed it, it was six o'clock, and all the village was on the move. Framed in the open doorway great golden wagons went swaying down the cobbled street, followed by soft-padding strings of tasselled donkeys, the sun shining red through their ears.

As I stood ready to leave, I heard a shout behind me : 'Where is he ? Where is the stranger ?' – and Doña Maria strode forth, wildly disarrayed from her bed, and thrust a handful of figs into my shirt. 'Say nothing of that. Nothing at all,' she growled. 'What a night the old one had.' I gave her the coppers I owed her, and she considered them distractedly for a moment, weighing them in her hand as if about to return them. Then she changed her mind, popped them under her skirt, slapped me on the back, and wished me good-bye.

Down by the river, under an olive tree, a group of girls were drawing water. The girl from the inn was among them, and their voices rang sharp, like a clashing of knives on stone. As I came down the lane their chattering stopped, and they turned their heads all together to watch me. Caught in this alert, surprised, almost pastoral attitude, they offered me an unblinking cluster of eyes, intent and expressionless as the eyes of calves, and desolating too. I padded past quickly, and nobody moved, but their eyes followed me like the eyes in a painting. I remember their blank shining pupils, like pebbles in water. The girl from the inn gave no sign that she knew me.

Out in the plain once more, head down to the dust, I walked fast to make the most of the morning. Not that I'd any particular need to hurry, but the girls had unsettled me to the point of believing that a little hard walking would balance the mind. After a couple of hours or so, still in the grip of a romantic melancholy, I stopped by a little roadside shrine, which announced that a boy, aged ten, had been killed on this spot by a madman, and asked travellers to pray for them both.

I ate the cool green figs which Doña Maria had given me, then walked on for another hour. The monotony of the plain, and the height of the wheat around me, restricted the view to only a few yards, so that I was unprepared for the sudden appearance of Toro – an ancient, eroded, red-walled town spread along the top of a huge flat boulder. The plain ended here in a series of geological convulsions that had thrown up gigantic shelves of rock, raw red in colour and the size of islands, rising abruptly to several hundred feet. Perched on one of the sharpest of these, and scattered along its crumbling edge, Toro looked like dried blood on a rusty sword. The cliff dropped sheer to the bed of the river and was littered with the debris of generations.

Clambering up to the town, in the hard noon silence, I was

ready to find it deserted, or to see some Pompeii-like waste long blasted by doom and inhabited only by cats and asses. On the contrary – half-ruined though it certainly was – the town was buzzing with life, with whitewashed hovels brimming with rackety families, children running through holes in the walls, busy shops and cafés flourishing behind broken-down doors, and the streets crowded with elegant walkers.

I sat in a chair outside the Café Español and watched the parade go by. Each strolling young man was a pocket dandy, carefully buttoned in spite of the heat; each girl a crisp, freshly laundered doll, flamboyantly lacy around neck and knees; and it was curious to see so much almost Edwardian fashion blooming on such an arid shelf of rock. A public show of clothes was obviously the first thing here, in spite of the poverty and ruin of the place, where the poorest tin shack seemed to produce its immaculate debutante, picking her way casually among the offal, superbly dressed for display by a busy task-force of aunts sewing and ironing behind the scenes.

As I sat there watching I was approached by a thin young man who snatched off his beret and bowed.

'I am Billette, mister – at your orders,' he said; then he stood by my chair and waited. He wore a tattered blue suit which seemed to cover his limbs like a cobweb, and his hand clutched a sheaf of tickets.

I offered him a drink, and he sat down beside me, apologizing for any derangement. Then, with a twopenny beer in his hand, he became officially my friend and interpreter of the scene before me. Speaking slowly, carefully, with icy detachment, he indicated the passing dandies.

'Señoritos!' he said. 'From the University of Valladolid. Lawyers and doctors every one. We have many of them. But it makes no difference. We are still ruined, and die.'

Clutching his glass with long spatulate fingers, he shivered and blinked at the sunlight. Why had I come to Toro? I had the right, of course. The world was free for young 'Frenchmen' like me. Tonight, he said, the town would hold a holy procession; I ought to see it, but I should forgive him for mentioning it.

Then he pulled himself together. 'We are the strongest city in the plain,' he said, 'and also very holy. We have saints in the church more beautiful than anybody. The people lead sacred lives ... Look there, for instance.' He jerked his head dolefully and pointed up the street.

I saw a ten-year-old child, dressed like a bride, come mincing along the pavement – a wedding-cake toy capped with a halo of flowers and carrying lilies in her white-gloved hands. She advanced with jaunty solemnity, eyes demurely composed, accompanied by two large women in black, and when the sun fell on her she suddenly blazed like a starshell with a brilliant incandescent light.

'See her,' said Billette. 'Another virgin for the Carmelites. We offer one up almost every day.'

All down the street the child was embraced and saluted, while she dropped her eyes and tried to suppress her excitement; old men doffed their hats, mothers held babies towards her, children ran up and kissed her cheek.

'We are a holy town, as you see,' said my companion. 'Our girls marry Christ from the cradle. Where do they go? Into the caverns of the Church. We shan't see this one again.'

He may have been pulling my leg, of course; it was probably nothing more than her first communion. Yet as the child danced away among her dark attendants she seemed to leave an unhealthy flush behind her.

Throughout the afternoon I drowsed behind the café curtains, hiding from the worst of the heat. The streets were empty now except for a few thin dogs hugging the walls for an inch of shade. All else was silence, blinding white, while the sun moved high over the town, destroyer, putrifier, scavenger of the hovels and breeder of swarming ills.

At the first breath of evening I went off with Billette to look at the castle on the edge of the town. 'Morisco,' he explained; a bit of infidel terrorism now rapidly returning to dust ... He led me nimbly among the eroded dungeons – 'the sepulchres of the Cristianos' – whose bones, he said, were now in the church (and seemed to be lavishly surrounded with excrement).

Here I was approached by another young man who had been

poking distractedly among the ruins – a slim womanish figure, wielding a gold-topped cane and carrying a portfolio under his arm. He spoke in a delicate dancing language of his own, a kind of two-step between French and English. He was not from Toro, oh no! – a brutish place. (Billette stood listening with jealous incomprehension.) No, he was an art-master from Valencia, and exploited his leisure by executing ornamental lettering for churches. 'Regard!' he said sharply, and opened the portfolio to reveal some particularly lurid examples of his art. 'At this, I am known to be a master. But today I flower in a desert...'

Leaning against the crumbling ramparts and gazing at the river below us, he worked himself into a lather of bitterness, bewailing the age of profanity in which he was doomed to live, together with the cowardice of the modern Church. There was no taste, no reverence for ornamental lettering any more, at least not for such devotional work as his. They preferred the gaudy shams of the cheap printers of Madrid, which the Church was buying in bulk like stamps. Where were the bishops and cardinals of old? he cried, those patrons of artistic piety? the holy princes of Christendom whose sainted hands once raised the artist to the floors of Heaven?

Billette was clearly impressed by the noise the other was making and watched him with shining eyes, while the young man sighed, panted, and twisted his eloquent limbs into shuddering postures of outrage. How could he possibly live under such shame and neglect, and continue to keep up his little house in Valencia? Soon he would be reduced to such crimes as mottoes and calendars, which would kill his aged mother.

All this was in French and English. Billette gaped with admiration, recognizing the other's passion, if not the sense. Accepting the sound of protest as something he must obviously share, he touched the young man's arm and began to quieten and console him. A curious calm descended as they whispered together, leaning close in the setting sun. Then with an excuse they left me, and wandered off hand in hand, brothers of a momentary confusion.

*

Back in Toro the evening deepened with a hot green light as the town prepared for the coming procession. Huge banners and shawls swung down from the balconies, all decorated in Grand Guignol fashion, some stitched with black crosses, others tied at the corners with gigantic bows of crêpe. Townsfolk, and stove-hatted peasants from the plain, were already crowding along the pavements, some with small buttoned cushions and stools to kneel on, all gazing in silence up the street.

The bells, which for an hour had been crashing out a jangle of discords, suddenly stopped with a humming abruptness. At this signal the multitude went quite still, fixing its eyes on the distant church. A heap of gold at noon, it was now a dark blue shadow, hanging in the air like a wisp of incense. The silence increased, and even the cries of the children began instinctively to smother themselves. Then the doors were thrown open on to a sparkling darkness, like a cave full of summer fireflies, as several hundred candles streamed away from the altar and came fluttering towards the street.

Slowly, to the sound of a drum and trumpet, the shuffling procession emerged, and the crush of spectators standing nearest the church fell to their knees as though they'd been sprayed with bullets. The dry beat of the drum and naked wail of the trumpet sounded as alien as I could wish, conjuring up in the glow of this semi-African twilight an extraordinary feeling of fear and magic.

Was it the death of their saint they were so lugubriously celebrating with their black banners and dripping candles? Her image came riding high in the heart of the procession, a glittering figure of painted wood, bobbing her crowned head stiffly, left and right, to the kneeling crowds in the gutters. Her bearers sweated under their jewelled load, grunting patiently into their lacy shirt-fronts, while two lines of young women scuffled along behind, nasally chanting some tuneless dirge.

As the image approached us, protestations and tears rose spontaneously from the crowd around me. Then the saint drew level and I saw her face, rose-tinted, pretty as a sugared sweet, with the smooth head perched on a little doll-like body heavily tented in robes of velvet.

Whoever she was, this prim painted mannikin dominated the town with an undeniable presence, and as she passed on her way she seemed to trail behind a gigantic swathe of absolution. Praise, thanks, and supplication followed her, passionately uttered by young and old. Clearly, to all eyes, she was the living Saint, Sister of the Virgin, Intimate of Christ, Eternal Mediator with the Ghost of God and Compassionate Mother of Toro.

With a dying cry in the distance the image passed from sight, the drum and the trumpet faded, and the last of the girls shuffled by, their candles wilting and guttering, leaving behind in the street the spent faces of the peasants, a smell of wax, burnt wick, and exhaustion. There was a short hushed pause, then the heavy soul-laden blanket was lifted like a cloud from the town. Suddenly everyone was nodding and smiling at one another, gathering up their children and cushions, and remarking how well the Saint had looked today – so comely, so linda, such an excellent colour – and making ready to enjoy themselves.

The solemn wake was over. The streets filled immediately with promenaders spreading from wall to wall. The lights were switched on – strings of small coloured bulbs that looped everywhere like skeins of fruit – and all the life of Toro began to pass beneath them, up and down and around, friend shown to friend, foe to foe, wife to lover, each to all. For a while I wandered invisibly among them, submerged by their self-absorption; and suddenly found myself wishing for a face I knew, for Stroud on a Saturday night . . .

The next day I remember only vaguely. It was one of the hottest of that Spanish summer. No doubt I should have stayed at the inn till the worst was over, but the journey had become a habit.

Toro was deserted when I left it, its shutters still drawn, and a brassy glare hung over the plain. The road ran through the wheat as straight as a meridian, like a knife-cut through a russet apple, and I followed it east towards the morning sun, which was already huge and bloated. After a while, being out-doors became a hallucination, and one felt there was no longer any air to breathe, only clinkered fumes and blasts of sulphur that seemed to rise through cracks in the ground. I remember stopping for water at silent farms where even the dogs were too exhausted to snarl, and where the water was scooped up from wells and irrigation ditches and handed to me warm and green.

The violence of the heat seemed to bruise the whole earth and turn its crust into one huge scar. One's blood dried up and all juices vanished; the sun struck upwards, sideways, and down, while the wheat went buckling across the fields like a solid sheet of copper. I kept on walking because there was no shade to hide in, and because it seemed to be the only way to agitate the air around me. I began to forget what I was doing on the road at all; I walked on as though keeping a vow, till I was conscious only of the hot red dust grinding like pepper between my toes.

By mid-morning I was in a state of developing madness, possessed by pounding deliriums of thirst, my brain running and reeling through all the usual obsessions that are said to accompany the man in the desert. Fantasies of water rose up and wrapped me in cool wet leaves, or pressed the thought of cucumber peel across my stinging eyes and filled my mouth with dripping moss. I began to drink monsoons and winter mists, to lick up the first fat drops of thunder, to lie down naked on deep-sea sponges and rub my lips against the scales of fish. I saw the steamy, damp-uddered cows of home planting their pink-lily mouths in the brook, then standing, knee-deep among dragonflies, whipping the reeds with their tasselled tails. Images bubbled up green from valleys of shining rain and fields of storm-crushed grass, with streams running down from the lime-cold hills into buttery swamps of flowers. I heard my mother again in her summer kitchen splashing water on garden salads, heard the gulping gush of the garden pump and swans' wings beating the lake . . .

The rest of the day was a blur. I remember seeing the spire of a church rising from the plain like the jet of a fountain.

Then there was a shower of eucalyptus trees brushing against a roadside tavern, and I was at a bar calling for bottles of pop.

'No, no! You mustn't drink. You will fall down dead.' The woman threw up her hands at the sight of me, then turned, alarmed, to shout at a couple of well-dressed gentlemen eating radishes at a table in the corner.

The older man bowed. '*Alemán? Francais?* The lady is right – you are too hot for drinking.'

'He will drop at our feet. Just look at his face.' Everybody tutted and shook their heads.

I could only stand there croaking, desperate with thirst. Somebody gave me some ice to suck. Then I was told to rest and cool off, while they asked me the usual questions : where I came from, where I was going.

At my reply, the woman threw up her hands again. 'On foot? It is not to be thought of!' The gentlemen started an argument, spitting out radishes at each other like furious ex-clamations. 'If he's English, he's the first walking Englishman I've seen,' said one. 'They walk all over the place,' said the other. 'Up and down mountainsides. Round and round the poles.' 'Yes, yes – but they do not walk in Spain.'

I heard their voices fading and booming around me. My head felt feverish, tight, and bursting. Then someone was leaning over me. 'Enough of the excremental walking. Holy Mother of God, give the young man a little drink. If he lives, and still wishes to go to the city, we will take him in the car.'

The first mouthful of mineral water burst in my throat and cascaded like frosted stars. Then I was given a plate of ham, several glasses of sherry, and a deep languor spread through my limbs. I remember no more of my benefactors, or what they said; only the drowsy glories of drinking. Later, much later, I was lifted to my feet and half-led, half-carried outside. Then, stretched fast asleep in the back of the car, I was driven like a corpse to Valladolid.

# 5. Valladolid

Valladolid: a dark square city hard as its syllables – a shut box, full of the pious dust and preserved breath of its dead whose expended passions once ruled a world which now seemed of no importance. The motor car had dropped me in the middle of it, on this evening of red stale dust, to find myself surrounded by churches and crypt-like streets bound by the rigidity of six-teenth-century stone. There was little life to be seen in the listless alleys, and the street lamps were hooded by a mysterious thickness of the light. I felt once again the unease of arriving at night in an unknown city – that faint sour panic which seems to cling to a place until one has found oneself a bed.

I stood for a while in the plaza, resting my knapsack against a wall and recovering from the fevered stupors of the day. Silent rope-soled creatures passed shadowless by. I was oppressed by the heavy vacuum around me. This was one of the major cities of Castilla la Vieja – a name ringing with cold chisels and chains. It was here, a priest told me later, that Marghanita de Jarandilla looked from her prison tower and wept tears of gold into the laps of beggars; and it was here, to the altar of San Martin, that a poor cripple from Vallaverde crawled with his severed leg and carved a magnificent crucifix out of the bone. A city of expired fanaticisms and murdered adorations – of the delicate and elaborate Moors, of Ferdinand and Isabella, of the deceived Columbus, and the gentle, crisp-brained Cervantes. Against the lives of all these rose the present darkness, the gloom of the drawn oven, the cold closed lamp.

Night was on this city, and upon me too. So I went off to look for a bed. Down a narrow lane I suddenly came on the barracks – a great pile of medieval granite. Groups of ragged young conscripts lay about on the pavement, crouching in hazy circles of lamplight, scratching, spitting, playing tattered cards, and passing their penniless time. I asked them where I might find a lodging, and they pointed across the road.

'Try the Borracho,' said one.

'An ogre,' said another.

'But don't mind him. He's got beds of brass.'

I found the Borracho sitting in a filthy room swilling wine from a goat-skin bag. A naked child lay asleep on the table beside him with its head pillowed in a half-cut pumpkin. The Borracho had spiky grey hair and the looks of a second murderer. His face was as dark and greasy as a pickled walnut and a moustache curled round his lip like an adder.

I asked for a bed, and he just glowered at me.

'Go sleep in the river,' he said.

He took another loud drink, wiped the wine-bag across his mouth, slumped in his chair, and closed his eyes. When he opened them again and saw me still standing there, he struck the table, flapped his arms, and cried : 'Shoo !'

But I wouldn't budge. It was almost midnight now, and all I wanted to do was sleep. I repeated my question and the man suddenly crumpled up and quite childishly began to cry. His fleshy lips curled back and he grizzled like an infant, looking piteously about him for comfort. I offered him a cigarette and he took it between his long black nails, without looking at it, and ripped it down the middle. Then rolling tobacco and paper into a neat little ball, he popped them into his mouth.

'What about a bed then ?' I asked.

He looked at me with hatred, but eventually got to his feet.

'There's only one,' he said. 'And may you be pleased to die in it.' And he jerked his head towards the door.

The narrow stairs dripped with greasy mysterious oils and had a feverish rotten smell. They seemed specially designed to lead the visitor to some act of depressed or despairing madness. I climbed them with a mixture of obstinacy and dread, the Borracho wheezing behind me. Half-way up, in a recess, another small pale child sat carving a potato into the shape of a doll, and as we approached she turned, gave us a quick look of panic, and bit off its little head.

The brass bed was magnificent, as the soldiers had promised, and stood about six feet high, with knobs on. It was the only piece of furniture in a room which otherwise seemed to have been devastated by violent tenants. The light from the street lamps decorated the walls with liquid dilating shapes, and the young soldiers were still visible on the pavement outside, some of them fast asleep. The Borracho had recovered his truculence and threw the key at my feet, demanding the rent in advance. Then he fished in his pocket, gave me a candle-end, and said he didn't mind if I burnt down the house.

When he'd gone, I sat on the bed and swung my feet and ate my last bit of bread and cheese. I was feeling easier now, in spite of the savagery of the place. I was established. I had a room in this city.

I was awakened next morning by the high clear voice of a boy singing in the street below. The sound lifted me gradually with a swaying motion as though I was being cradled on silken cords. It was cool crisp singing, full-throated and pure, and surely the most painless way to be wakened – and as I lay there listening, with the sun filtering across me, I thought this was how it should always be. To be charmed from sleep by a voice like this, eased softly back into life, rather than by the customary brutalities of shouts, knocking, and alarm-bells like blows on the head. The borders of consciousness are anxious enough, raw and desperate places; we shouldn't be dragged across them like struggling thieves as if sleep was a felony.

The boy was leaning against a lamp-post beneath the barrack walls and carrying a basket slung over his shoulders. He was about twelve years old, thin, and scrub-headed, and was obviously singing for what he could get. But he sang with the whole of his body, his eyes tight-closed, his bare throat rippling in the sunlight, and his voice had a nasal wail that obliterated the city around him – the voice of Islam, aimed at the sky and pitched to an empty landscape. Unshaven soldiers, half-dressed and quiet, leaned listening from the barrack windows. Some of them threw him bits of bread and slices of orange, and when he'd finished he gathered them up in the basket.

Valladolid had a better face this morning. The mask of red dust had been wiped away in the night and an innocent radiance glittered over the heavy buildings. The sky was a blank hard blue, almost chemically bright, stretched for another day of heat. I bought a handful of fruit and collected some letters from the post office, then found a café down by the fishmarket. As I ate my breakfast I opened my letters, which were the first I'd received in Spain. I was surrounded by stale odours of melting ice, by housewives with dripping baskets, by banks of prawns and the dead eyes of fish, each one an ocean sealed and sunless. My letters from home spoke of whist-drives and marrows, of serene and distant gossip. But none of them called me back and it looked as though I was here for good. The time had come for me to make some money.

I'd been told that street-fiddlers in Spain would need a licence – though not every city demanded it. So off I went, after breakfast, to the city hall, which looked like a bankrupt casino. Soldiers with fixed bayonets sat around on the stairs, and hungry dogs ran in and out like messengers, while the usual motionless queues of silent peasants waited for officials who would never appear. Doubting that there would be a queue for fiddlers that morning, I climbed the stairs and opened the first door I came to.

The room inside was large and crowded with heavy presidential furniture. At a desk by the window sat a reed-thin man – or rather he inclined himself parallel to it, his feet on a cabinet, a cigar in his mouth, and a chessboard across his knees. I could see his long hooked profile, like a Leonardo drawing, and one pensive downcast eye. He moved a few pawns and hummed a little, then swung in his chair towards me – and his face, seen front-on, almost disappeared from view, so unusually thin he was. I was aware of two raised eyebrows and an expression of courtly inquiry which seemed entirely unsupported by flesh.

'You are lost, perhaps?'

'I'd like to see the Mayor,' I said.

'So would I. So would all the world.'

'Is he away?'

The man giggled, and a convulsion ran up his body like an air-bubble up a spout.

'Yes, he's away. He's gone to the madhouse.'

I said I was sorry, but he raised his hand.

'Oh, no. He is happy. Who wouldn't be in such a place? Biscuits and chocolate at all hours of the day. Nuns to talk to, and coloured wool to play with ... At least, so they say.' He looked secretively at his cigar. 'But you see me here. If I can help ...'

When I told him what I wanted, he gave a little musical squeak and his eyebrows jumped with pleasure.

'How charming,' he murmured. 'But of course you shall. One moment – Manolo, please!'

A swarthy young man, dressed in trousers and pyjama-top, entered softly from another room.

'Find me a licence, Manolito.'

'What kind of licence?'

'Oh, any kind. Only make it a nice one.'

'Then permit me, Don Ignacio.' The young man grasped his chief by the legs, hoisted them from the cabinet, and searched the papers beneath them. Meanwhile Don Ignacio reclined indolently, his legs stuck in the air, beaming upon me and singing 'rumpty-dum-diddle'.

'To sell water,' murmured the clerk. 'To erect a small tomb . . . to beat gold . . . to press juniper berries . . . ah, here we have it, I do believe. Don Ignacio, with your permission . . .'

He replaced his chief's legs on the cabinet and handed him a kind of finely engraved cheque-book, together with pen and ink. Don Ignacio doubled up and began to write, rolling his tongue and grunting with effort. Delicate scrolls and decorations ran over the paper, feathery tendrils in violet ink; then the thing was finished, dusted and sealed, and signed with a delicious flourish.

'There,' said Don Ignacio. 'The city is yours. Rumpty-dum-diddle-de-ay.'

I studied my licence and was pleased with it. It looked like a Royal Charter. Headed with an engraving of lions and a scarlet seal, it formally proclaimed: 'THAT, by using the powers attributed to and conferred upon the Mayorality, and by virtue of the precepts of the Municipal Bye-laws and the appropriate tariffs due to the said most Excellent Ayuntamiento; a licence is hereby granted to Don Lorenzo Le, that he may walk and offer concerts through the streets of this City, and the public squares of the same, PROVIDED ALWAYS that he does not in any manner cause riot, demonstrations, or prejudice the free movement of traffic and persons . . .'

'That will be half a peseta,' said Don Ignacio mildly, swinging his feet back on to the top of the desk. Then he invited me to join him in a game of chess, the question of the fee was forgotten.

*

Later, armed with my licence, I went back to the Borracho's to
fetch my violin and get to work. A woman was scrubbing the
courtyard, and she straightened up as I entered and raised an
arm to push back her hair. Her handsome, muddy, exhausted
face showed that she was expecting someone else. 'Have you
seen him?' she asked. I shook my head, and her eyes went grey
and listless. To get to my room I had to step over three naked
children who sat weeping in pools of water. Even in his
absence the deadly stench of the Borracho permeated the place
like gas.

After repairing my fiddle, and dusting off the new straw hat
which I'd bought in Zamora market, I went out – for the first
time in a Spanish town – to try my luck in the streets. I found
a busy lane, placed my hat on the ground, and struck up a
rusty tune. According to my experience in England, money
should then have dropped into the hat; but it didn't work out
that way here. No sooner had I started to play than everybody
stopped what they were doing and gathered round me in a
silent mass, blocking the traffic, blotting out the sun, and treading my new hat into the ground. Again and again I fished it
from under their feet, straightened it out, and moved somewhere else. But as soon as I struck up afresh, the crowd re-
formed and encircled me, and I saw in their scorched brown
faces an expression I was soon to know well – a soft relaxed
childishness and staring pleasure, an abandonment of time to a
moment's spectacle. .

This was all very well, but I was making no money – and
there was scarcely room even to swing my arm. Every so often
I was compelled to break off, and to attempt a wheedling
speech, begging the multitude to have the kindness to walk up
and down just a little, or at least to draw back and reveal my
hat. A number of lounging soldiers, half-understanding, began
to shout what I said at the others. The others screamed back,
telling them to shut up and listen. In the meantime, nobody
moved.

Presently a policeman appeared, his unbuttoned tunic revealing a damp and hairy chest. He had a dirty rifle slung over his
shoulder and was sucking a yellow toothpick.

'German?'

'No, English.'

'Licence?'

'Yes.'

He gave it a slumberous, heavy-lidded glance. Then, shifting his gun to his other shoulder, he hooked my hat on to the toe of his boot, kicked it high in the air, caught it, shook it, and turned crossly upon the crowd.

'Have you no shame?' he demanded. 'Or are you beggars of this town? Look, not a penny, not a dried garbanzo. Have you no dignity to be standing here? Either pay, or go.'

Giggling uneasily, the crowd backed away. There was the tinkle of a coin on the pavement. The policeman picked it up, dropped it into the hat, and handed it to me with a bow.

'Milk from dry udders,' he said loftily. 'You are welcome. Now please continue . . .'

I did so for a while, not made too happy by his support, while he held back the crowd with his gun. But from then on I used the trick which I'd learned in Southampton – I made sure the hat was properly baited beforehand. Nobody kicked over a hat with pennies in it, they just stood delicately around the brim. I learned some other lessons, too. That men were less responsive than women – unless approached in a café, when they paid with the gestures of noblemen. That any Spanish tune worked immediately, and called up ready smiles, while any other kind of music – Schubert excepted – was met by blank stares and bewilderment. Most important of all, I learned when to stop and move on, to spread myself around – a lesson taught me by a bootblack no higher than my knee who had been on the edge of the crowd all morning.

'You play much,' he said finally.

'Why, is it no good?'

'Good enough – but much, too much. Play less for the money. A couple of strophes will do. Then you will reach more people during the day.'

He was right, of course, especially where pavement cafés were concerned, whose clients liked a continuously changing scene. It was enough to make oneself known, followed by a quick whip round, and then to go off somewhere else.

At midday I stopped, having made about three pesetas. The heat by now was driving everyone indoors. So I bought a bottle of wine and a bag of plums and took them down by the river. There, under the mulberry trees, where some thin grass grew, I sat watching the slow green flow of the water. The shade from the trees lay on my hands and legs like pieces of cool wet velvet, and all sounds ceased, save for the piercing stutter of the cicadas which seemed to be nailing the heat to the ground.

I drowsed off presently with a half-eaten plum in my hand, and the bottle of wine untasted. Spanish afternoon-sleep was new to me, and I woke dazed, my limbs glutted with stupor. It was about five o'clock. A girl was wading in the river, her brown legs shining like caramel; while on the opposite bank, in a cloud of red dust, a boy was driving some mules to drink.

The hours had been eaten away, and evening had started, but I was content to lie where I was, to watch the drinking mules, and the girl in the river, and the boy, who was watching the girl. She walked gracefully, thigh-deep, balancing some washing on her head, while the boy stood on one leg leaning against a stick. He began to call out and taunt her, and the girl answered back, and their voices were sharp as the cries of moorhens. The cries continued for a while, bouncing hard on the water, almost visible in the dark red light; then suddenly the shouting ceased, and the girl turned in the river and began to cross to the other side, wading strong and deep towards the waiting boy, her short legs stockinged with mud ...

I went back to the town that evening in a mood of gauzy unreality, of vague unthinking enchantment. I remember kicking a melon along the street and feeling the air brush round my body. I wandered idly about in a state of aimless benignity, loving all things, even this baleful city – with its rancid shadows and scabby dogs, sweating pavements and offal-filled gutters; its blue-smocked ancients, remote as coolies; its children dozing in doorways, and its women surrounded by aromas of cooking fat, lemons, and chemical violets. I played no music that night, but went from bar to bar, drinking glasses of clotted wine. I was feverish, drowsy, and sentimental. I still had a touch of the sun.

The following morning the light-headedness continued, a curious suspension of focus. I returned to the market for breakfast, among sudden uproars and silences, with church-bells kicking in the throbbing towers. Eating bread and sausage, my back to the church wall, I was aware only of this point of time, the arrested moment of casual detail, the unsorted rubbish of now. I felt the heat of the sun dampened by draughts of ice blowing from fish-boxes stacked nearby. I remember a yawning cat – a pin-cushion of teeth and whiskers – sitting on a palm leaf in the gutter. A man said 'Good morning' and passed out of my life, stepping on a petal as though extinguishing a match. I saw an empty wine-barrel roll out of a tavern door, turn slowly, and roll back in again. I saw a hole in the road suddenly wink like a cyclops as a shadow flowered in and out of it. A boy lifted his shirt and scratched his belly, a house-wife picked up and put down an orange, and a mule stopped in the road, looked straight into my face, and wrinkled up his wet brown-papery nostrils.

For several more days the city moved somnambulantly before me, like a series of engravings seen through watery glass. I worked the streets and cafés, and made a few pesetas, but I knew I would not stay long. Its alternate elations and leaden ugliness set up uneasy hallucinations. Particularly of the poverty and waste symbolized by that mass of young conscripts gasping away their summer in the city barracks.

Locked up all day, peering from the narrow windows, or drilled to exhaustion on the burning square, in the evenings they were released in stupefied droves to possess the half-empty town. Across the plaza – an arena of silted tramlines – they shuffled like clowns in their crumpled khaki, circling, heads down, with nothing to spend or do, imprisoned by ennui and simple lust. In their cardboard boots they clumped up and down, kicking idly at invisible obstructions. Some languished in groups under the feeble lamps, sucking dead fags among the whirling flies. A few, the lucky ones, stood with tense sick faces

fingering the tin jewellery around the necks of their girls. But
the rest, the majority, without cigarettes or girls, just stood
where they were and whistled – making that sad thin sound
which is the sign of young soldiers everywhere, standing about
in shut streets on rainy Sundays, on midnight platforms where
no trains come, guarding forgotten dumps in abandoned bases
or empty petrol-tins in a desert – the sound of their wish to
be anywhere but there, the breath of the pointless hours expir-
ing.

Living at the Borracho's, across the street from the barracks,
I saw much of these scarecrow troops. I saw the garbage they
fed on, the way their youth was humbled, the way they were
condemned to spend their time. Bug-hunting, stealing, gambling
with thirds of a farthing, quarrelling, bled grey with boredom –
sometimes, perhaps, soothed by a lucky friendship, stretched
quietly with another boy; or seeking solitary relief in a jog-trot
of poetry, or a sudden ejaculation of sex-choked song. Or,
when pressures grew too great, going down in the dark to the
river to press a whore to the hard wet gravel, then returning
barefooted, ready for jail, having paid with their cardboard
boots.

Soldiers, priests, and an outer fringe of beggars – three silent
and separate categories; there were times at night, with the red
dust blowing in from the plain, when there seemed to be no
one else but these in the city. The soldiers and beggars groped
among the great blank buildings, invisible to each other's
miseries, invisible also to the sleek black priests slipping down
alleys like padded cats.

But the beggars I remember as something special to Valladolid, something it had nursed to a peak of malformation and
horror. One saw little of them by day; they seemed to be let
out only at night, surreptitiously, like mad relations. Then
limping, scuffling, hopping, and creeping, they came slowly out
of the shadows, advancing towards one at pavement-level to a
rhythmic chanting of moans and whispers. Here were old men,
youths and shrivelled children; creatures of every imagin-
able curse and deformity – blind, dumb, without hands,

without feet, covered with sores, dragging their bodies like sacks.

There was almost nothing for them in the streets except to act out their mutilations, sightlessly begging the empty air, holding up stumps of arms, pointing to empty eye-sockets, wrapping and unwrapping the worst of their sores. The children were especially quiet, mute concentrations of martyrdom, unable to envisage the stretch of doom ahead. They stood numbly apart, gazing through red-filmed eyes and holding out tiny wrinkled palms.

Young and old were like emanations of the stifling medievalism of this pious and cloistered city; infected by its stones, like the pock-marked effigies of its churches, and part of one of the more general blasphemies of Spain.

My last night in Valladolid sustained the sick fever of the place. Too hot to sleep, I stayed late in the bars and got rid of most of my money; then, about two in the morning, I went back to the inn to find it in a state of uproar.

The huge front door had been ripped from its hinges and lay in splinters across the street. The three youngest children were huddled inside, half naked, moaning with fear – while the Borracho's wife, storm centre of the scene, stood screaming at the foot of the stairs. Previously I'd only seen her as a listless drudge, now she was roused to a terrible stature, brandishing a spade in her hand like a two-edged sword, her eyes mad-yellow and full of sparks.

She turned towards me as I entered and made a blind gesture of fury, holding the spade out in front of her.

'I will kill him!' she cried. 'He is bad – bad!'

One of the children ran towards her, pressing against her legs, and she looked down at it with a squinting, distracted gaze as though she'd never seen it before.

'He comes home like a pig, and I lock him out. But he breaks down the door and tries to love Elvira – ELVIRA!' She turned suddenly and screamed out the name, beating the ground with the flat of the spade. 'Daughter! Daughter! . . .' The spade rang like a bell. 'I will smash his cojones against his teeth!'

'Where is he?' I said.

She looked savagely up the stairs and went mad again, beating the walls with frenzy.

'Are you dead yet?' she screamed. 'You prince of pigs! Shame of fathers throughout the world . . .'

She stood there shaking, her face green in the lamplight, the sweat glistening in her tangled hair. I took the spade from her hands, and was surprised how easily she surrendered it. Then I left her and went upstairs.

I found the Borracho on the landing, about half-way up, sprawled on his back, wet with blood and wine. He lay like a slaughtered bull, breathing in painful gasps and weeping to himself in the dark.

'Help me,' he whimpered.

I dragged him across to my room, and lit a candle. One side of his face was smashed and bleeding. I sponged and cleaned him as best I could, covered him with a coat, and went to bed.

The room, the house, the whole of the city, seemed suddenly corroded with misery. The Borracho lay on the floor, phlegm bubbling in his throat, drunkenly whispering his daughter's name.

# 6. Segovia—Madrid

There are certain places one leaves never expecting to see again, and I don't even wish to return to that city. I rose at dawn and went to the patio pump and washed it from my hands and face. Then with my bags on my back I passed through the damp flushed streets and entered once more into the open country.

Where should I go now? It didn't matter. Anywhere south

would do. Segovia, Madrid, the heart of Castille lay before me, and that was the direction I took. After the shuttered town, the landscape seemed to have broken from prison and rolled free and glittering away. Green oaks like rocks lay scattered among the cornfields, with peasants chest-deep in the wheat. It was the peak of harvest, and figures of extraordinary brilliance were spread across the fields like butterflies, working alone or in clusters, and dressed to the pitch of the light – blue shirts and trousers, and with broad gold hats tied with green and scarlet cloths. Submerged in the wheat, sickles flickered like fish, with rhythmic flashes of blue and silver; and as I passed, men straightened and shielded their eyes, silently watching me go, or a hand was raised in salute, showing among its sun-black fingers the glittering sickle like a curved sixth nail.

After the cramped shames of the city it was like a gulp of pure water to be back in this open landscape, in the rustling silence of the naked plain, its heaving solitude of raw burnt light.

Then, towards evening, I came to a village of mud – little more than a tumble of earth in a gulley. Few of the houses were whole, few had glass in their windows, most of the roofs were stuffed with sacking. They stood broken and bandaged, half-supporting each other like survivors from an old lost war.

The door of the inn this time was simply patched with a sheep-hurdle, and a wolfhound lay across the threshold. When the innkeeper appeared I asked if I could stay the night.

'The world is free,' he said. 'Why not?'

He gave me a loaf, and a rusty tin of sardines which I cut open with my knife. Two shabby Civil Guards were playing cards in a corner, their guns spread out on the table. Fat pink faces, small black eyes, cheating and quarrelling, they watched me darkly. When I'd finished my supper I began to write some notes, which they seemed to consider an act of reckless defiance. Throwing down their cards and picking up their guns they strode noisily across to my table. The notebook was snatched from my hand, sniffed at, shaken, thumped hard, and held upside down. A volley of questions followed, baffled and truculent. What was all this? they asked. They didn't like the

look of it. Where was I from? – and where were my docu-
ments? Speak up! I had much to answer for. A muddy half-
hour was spent in this oafish wrangle, while the innkeeper
watched us from a hole in the wall. Finally my indecipherable
writing, and the stupidity of my replies, drove them glowering
back to their corner.

I had already learned to be wary of the Civil Guards, who
were the poison dwarfs of Spain. They would suddenly ride
down upon you on their sleek black horses, far out in the open
country, and crowd around you, all leather and guns, and put
you through a bullying interrogation. Most of them were
afraid, and lived in a social vacuum which could only be filled
with violence; they had few friends in this country and were
suspicious of strangers and indeed of anyone on the road.
When challenged by one of them, I took deliberate pains never
to allow the issue to become clear between us; for they were
alarmed by confusion, and by their superiors, and could
usually be relied on to melt away rather than be caught in a
complicated situation with a foreigner.

So for the rest of the night these two left me alone. I wrote,
and they drank and quarrelled. Finally the landlord brought me
over a glass of brandy, and said that the world was free and he
only wished he could write. An innocent remark, but made
with a twisted mouth, and loud enough for the Guards to hear.

I'd been almost a month on the road since I landed at Vigo, and
was now finding the going better. At first I'd hobbled, but my
blisters had hardened and at last I could walk without pain. I
developed a long loping stride which covered some twenty
miles a day, an easy monotonous pace – slightly faster than the
mule-trains strung along the route, though slower than trotting
asses. On these straight Spanish roads, so empty of motor cars,
we moved between horizons like ships at sea, often remaining
for hours within sight of each other, gradually losing or gaining
ground. The mule-trains at that time were the caravans of
Castille, one of the threads of the country's life – teams of
small tasselled animals drawing high blue carts brightly painted
with vines and flowers. As gaudy as barges or wedding floats,

mounted on squealing five-foot wheels, they worked from city to city at three miles an hour – a rhythm unchanged since the days of Hannibal – carrying charcoal, firewood, wineskins, olives, oil, old iron, and gossip. The drivers were a race apart, born and bred on the road, and recognizable by their flat, almost Siberian faces. With long whips and short legs, they travelled like Arabs, some with boys to look after their comforts, and slept at noon in hammocks slung between the wheels, rocking gently to the pace of the mules, and then spent their nights round fires among the open rocks or wrapped in harness in the courtyards of inns. They were the hereditary newsbearers of the Spanish plains, old as the wheel and separate in their ways as gypsies.

I followed this straight southern track for several days, living on figs and ears of wheat. Sometimes I'd hide from the sun under the wayside poplars, face downwards, watching the ants. There was really no hurry. I was going nowhere. Nowhere at all but here. Close to the spicy warmth of this foreign ground a few inches away from my face. Never in my life had I felt so fat with time, so free of the need to be moving or doing. For hours I could watch some manic ant dragging a piece of orange peel through the grass, pushing and pulling against impossible barriers in a confused and directionless frenzy.

Then one day I noticed a long low cloud lifting slowly above the southern horizon, a purple haze above the quivering plain – the first sign of the approaching Sierras. After the monotonous wheatfields it was like a landfall, the distant coastline of another country, and as I walked, it climbed steadily till it filled half the sky – the immense east–west barrier of the Guadarramas.

Already cool winds were blowing down from its peaks, and the plain was lifting into little hills, and by the next afternoon I'd left the wheat behind me and entered a world of Nordic pinewoods. Here I slipped off the heat like a sweat-soaked shirt and slept an hour among the resinous trees – a fresh green smell as sweet as menthol compared with the animal reek of the plain. I noticed that each tree, slashed with a pattern of fishbone cuts, was bleeding gum into little cups. The wounded trunks seemed to be running with drops of amber, stinging the air with their piercing scent, while some of the older trees, bled dry and abandoned, curled in spirals like burning paper. But it was a good place to sleep; the wood was empty of flies, who had learnt to avoid its sticky snares, and the afternoon sun sucked up the flavour of each tree till the whole wood swam in incense like a church.

The villages in the foothills were full of flowers and fountains, but none of them had any food. I remember Cuéllar, Shulomonon, and Naval de Oro – places of steep craggy lanes and leaf-smothered towers and old doors pitted with gigantic keyholes. But all I got to eat from the lot of them was a piece of goat's cheese as hard as a stone.

I remember coming to one village whose streets were black with priests, and its taverns full of seething atheists. Some stood in a doorway heaving stones at the church, others sang obscenities about the bishop. Then a group cornered me in a tavern to complain about their Roman fountain – a naked goddess carved from local marble. Once, they said, she lay in the square, and jets of water sprang out of her breasts. Most beautiful to behold – but the priests had smashed her with hammers and buried her remains in the hills.

They were only shepherds, they said, but theirs was an artistic village; and they pointed out two pictures hanging on the tavern wall. Each was an original, painted on canvas, and the colour of uncooked meat: one was of a broken puppet, labelled 'The Show is Ended'; and the other of a sedate Victorian family, father, mother, and beribboned little girl, watching a dog bleed to death on the carpet. 'We love art, my beauty,' said one of the shepherds. Later, he tried to kiss me.

The wine in Shulomonon was raw and bitter, but cost less than a penny a glass. While sipping some of this, I met an English woman from Walsall, who had just spent five weeks touring Morocco with her husband. She looked worn out and bewildered. Her husband was asleep in the street. She asked for news of the Royal Family.

*

Early one evening I left the last of these villages and headed for Segovia, about six miles away. As I climbed the hill I saw some girls sitting in the mouth of a cave, facing the sunset, sewing and singing. 'My boy is sharp as salt,' they sang, 'with a house full of gold and silver . . .'

At this point I got a lift in a farmer's cart, which was loaded with sacks of chaff. As we lumbered along, the farmer talked about work and looked at my hands out of the corner of his eyes. 'It is different in some countries, I believe,' he said. 'But God gave us a country we must fight like a lion.' Suddenly he gave a loud cry, lashed the mules with his whip, and aimed the cart straight up the hillside, leaving the road altogether to follow some ancient track which climbed sheer among the boulders. The mules kicked and slithered, dug their hind-legs into the ground, and spread their haunches like thin black frogs, panting and straining, while the cart rocked like a ship and I clung to the farmer's belt. Half an hour later, with the wheels bouncing off rocks and the mules in a lather of sweat, we reached the top of the rise and saw the city below us, and the farmer locked the wheels for the downhill slide.

Segovia was a city in a valley of stones – a compact, half-forgotten heap of architectural splendours built for the glory of some other time. Here were churches, castles, and medieval walls standing sharp in the evening light, but all dwarfed by that extraordinary phenomenon of masonry, the Roman aqueduct, which overshadowed the whole. It came looping from the hills in a series of arches, some rising to over a hundred feet, and composed of blocks of granite weighing several tons and held together by their weight alone. This imperial gesture, built to carry water from a spring ten miles away, still strode across the valley with massive grace, a hundred vistas framed by its soaring arches, to enter the city at last high above the rooftops, stepping like a mammoth among the houses.

'The Aqueduct,' said the farmer, pointing with his whip, in case by chance I had failed to notice it. But to me, not having heard about it before, it came as a unique and visual shock.

'It's like a bridge,' he went on. 'You could drive across it. I once crossed it with a coach and horses.'

'Wouldn't it be too narrow?' I asked.

He looked at me sharply.

'I drove across it in a narrow coach.'

Entering the city by the Puerto de Santiago, the farmer gave me some carobs and wished me a good night's rest. I found an inn tucked away under the aqueduct, conveniently roofed by one of its arches – a vast cave-like place of naked granite smelling warmly of pigs and horses.

Segovia was mounted on rock and still partly boxed in by its Roman-Iberian walls, a small snug city of steep-stepping streets which seemed to ignore the invention of the wheel. There was time before supper to explore some of these alleys, dappled with pools of warm red lamplight, where naked children darted into their tattered houses like pheasants into nests of bracken. At close quarters, the aqueduct seemed both benevolent and mad, its jets of masonry vaulting the sky, and the huge blocked feet coming down on the town and throwing everything out of scale.

After a supper of beans and mutton, served in a cloud of woodsmoke, I was invited out into the plaza to watch a midnight ciné. Here, once again, the aqueduct came into use, with a cotton sheet strung from one of its pillars, on to which a pale beam of light, filtering from an opposite window, projected an ancient and jittery melodrama. Half the town, it seemed, had turned out for the show, carrying footstools and little chairs, while children swarmed on the rooftops and hung in clusters from the trees, their dark heads shining like elderberries.

The film's epic simplicity flickered across the Roman wall, vague and dim as a legend, but each turn of the plot was followed with gusto, people jumping up and down in their seats, bombarding the distant shadows with advice and warning, mixed with occasional shouts of outrage. The appearance of the villain was met by darts and stones, the doltish hero by exasperation, while a tide of seething concern was reserved for the plight of the heroine who spent a vigorously distressful time. During most of the film she hung from ropes in a tower, subject to the tireless affronts of the villain, but when the hero finally bestirred himself and disembowelled the villain with a knife, the audience was satisfied and went to bed.

I was not long in Segovia, and haven't been back there since, but I still recall some of its quieter melancholies – the cool depths of the Cathedral, clean and bare, full of wide and curving spaces, and the huge stained-glass windows hanging like hazed chrysanthemums in the amber distances of its height. Also the small black pigs running in and out of shop doorways – often apparently the only customers; and the storks roosting gravely on the chimney-pots, gazing across the valley like bony Arabs.

Then one afternoon, just outside the city walls, I found the little church of the local Virgin, a macabre memorial lying at the foot of the Peña Grajera – the desolate 'Cliff of Crows'. This granite rock, smothered with croaking birds, was also Segovia's cliff of blood, one of the many such places of easy death to be found on the edge of Spanish towns. From here, in the past, Segovia had been in the habit of tossing into the gorge its felons, adulterers, and heretics; thus suiting poverty and indolence by saving the price of a bullet or the extra effort of a sword-thrust. A strolling priest took pains to give me these local tit-bits, as well as to explain the significance of the birds on the cliff; pointing out that the slain, in any case, belonged to the world of the damned and that the crows were the ghosts of their godless souls.

The priest seemed drawn to this noisome place, and stayed with me for a while, gazing with a soft little smile at the fouled-up cliff where the birds rustled and flapped like bats. He mentioned the thirteenth-century heroine, Maria del Salto, a beautiful Jewess accused of adultery. 'Having been cast from the rock in the usual manner,' he said, 'she called on the Virgin to prove her innocence, and was compassionately halted while still in mid-air and allowed to float unhurt to the ground.' The little church in the gorge was built to commemorate the miracle – with no effect on later victims, apparently. But what I re-

member now is not the sedate little church, but the rock like a
bruise above it, its bloodstained face and exhausted crevices
haunted by the harsh dry voices of the birds.

Segovia left me with the echo of that carrion-infested place,
together with the hollow reverberations of the aqueduct. And
with one other, the last, as I walked out of the town and
passed the silent and shuttered bullring, and saw a white-faced
matador being carried to his car, weeping softly, attended by
whispering friends . . .

A few miles south of Segovia, at the foot of the Sierras, I
came on the royal gardens of La Granja – acres of writhing
statues, walks, and fountains rising from the dust like a mirage.
It was a grandiose folly, as large as Versailles and even more
extravagant, and I found it in the peak of bloom and entirely
deserted except for a few old gardeners with brooms.

A hundred fountains were playing, filling the sky with rain-
bows and creating an extraordinary dreamlike clamour. Marble
gods and wood-nymphs, dolphins and dragons, their anatomies
studded with pipes and nozzles, directed complex cascades at
one another or shot them high above the flowering trees.
Everything that could be done with water seemed to be going
on here, almost to the point of hydromania. Lakes, pools, jets,
and falls, flooded grottoes and exotic canals, all throbbed and
surged at different levels, reflecting classical arbours, paths, and
terraces, or running like cooling milk down the statuary.

Yet there was nobody to see it. Nobody but me – except, of
course, for the gardeners, who went shuffling about as though
under some timeless instruction, preparing for the return of
some long-dead queen.

I stayed in the gardens for an hour or more, furtively paddling among the trickling leaves. The fountains, I learned later,
played only on rare occasions, and I don't know why they
played that day. It was like the winding-up of some monarch's
toy, of which the owner had rapidly tired, and which now lay
abandoned at the foot of the mountain together with its aged
keepers. The fact was that La Granja, when looked at closely,
was more than a little vulgar – a royal inflation of a suburban
mind, a costly exercise with gnomes and toadstools.

*

It took me two days to cross the Sierra Guadarrama, as through another season and another country, climbing a magnificent road of granite blocks to a point almost two miles high. Here were racing brooks, great shadowy forests, and fallen boulders covered with flowering creepers. It seemed already autumn here; clouds rolled down the summits, dropping cool intermittent showers, while shepherds scrambled about, followed by wolf-like dogs, and the air smelt freshly of resin and honey.

I spent the first night in a grove of oak trees, lying on leaves as wet as Wales, under a heavy dew and a cold sharp moon and surrounded by the continuous bells of sheep. In the morning I woke shivering to eat a breakfast of goat's cheese, which the night had soaked and softened, then watched the sunlight move slowly down the trunks of the pine trees, dark red, as though they bled from the top. Nearby was a waterfall pouring into a bowl of rock, where I stripped and took a short sharp bathe. It was snow-cold, brutal, and revivifying, secluded among the trees, and when I'd finished I sat naked on a mossy stone, slowly drying in the rising sun. I seemed to be in a pocket of northern Europe, full of the cold splendour of Finnish gods. A green haze of pine-dust floated in shafts of sunlight and squirrels swung and chattered above me. Gulping the fine dry air and sniffing the pitch-pine mountain, I was perhaps never so alive and so alone again.

By midday I'd climbed to the six thousand feet pass of Puerto de Navacerrado, where I rested awhile under towering peaks that were dusted with summer snow. Great banks of cloud rolled up the northern slopes, broke over the ridges, and disappeared; while before me, through the pass, I saw a new country emerge – the immense plain of La Mancha, stretching flat as a cowhide and smudged like a sore with distant Madrid.

Crossing the Sierra was not just a stage on my journey, in spite of the physical barrier. It was also one of those sudden, jerky advances in life, which once made closes the past for ever. It was a frontier for me in more ways than one, and not till I'd passed it did I feel really involved in Spain.

The Sierra, like the moon, had two distinct faces : the north one aloof and cold in its shadow, a place of green thickets and

alpine silence, while to the south the mountain was just a raw
burnt rock, the cliffs stripped bare by the sun – which Madrid
seemed to use as a kind of backyard wall on which to scribble
slogans for coñac and nightclubs. The north side had a pastoral
stillness, a veiled purity and calm; while the blistered south,
though at least ten miles from the city, already reeked of the
waste of the streets.

Even so, I was impatient to reach Madrid, and hurried my
way towards it, stumbling down pathways of broken shale,
naked of grass or trees, while the peaks of the mountains slipped back into the clouds, sealing off all I had been till then. One
more night on the slopes, then I reached the main road – a
clutter of cafés, shacks, and tyre-dumps. And here I was given a
lift by two racy young booksellers who were driving a van
loaded with Latin missals. The young men, very gay, presented
me with their cards and pointed out all the brothels as we
bowled into Madrid; where they dropped me at last, at about
ten in the morning, in the heart of the city, the heart of
Spain.

Madrid struck me at first as being all tram-bells and wire, false
marble and delapidation. Counting London, it was only the
second major city I'd seen, and I slipped into it as into the
jaws of a lion. It had a lion's breath, too; something fetid and
spicy, mixed with straw and the decayed juices of meat. The
Gran Via itself had a lion's roar, though inflated, like a circus
animal's – wide, self-conscious, and somewhat seedy, and lined
with buildings like broken teeth.

These wide show-streets displayed all that pomp and vacuity
one associated with Latin-America – political parade-grounds
driven between wedding-cake mansions and bearing the names
of presidents, historical dates, and virtues. Close behind them
however ran the living lanes of the city, narrow alleys stuffed
with carts and beggars, with thin little housemaids and tubercu-
lar children, beautiful and covered with sores.

I went first to the Post Office to collect my letters, which I
found filed under 'E' for 'Esquire' – one from a newspaper with
a third prize for a poem, and one from my mother hoping my

feet were dry. Then I walked round the back-streets near the Puerta del Sol, looking for a likely inn, and found one at last, as old as Chaucer, with a cowshed in the cellar. The proprietor wrote my name in a big black book, copying it from my mother's envelope, then handed me a doorkey as large as a spade and said my room would cost sixpence a night.

By now it was noon, with almost everyone under cover, in the bars and moistly shaded cafés, at this hour when Madrid properly came into its own – a dewdrop on the grid-iron plain. Most other capitals, in such heat, would still have been an inferno of duty, full of damp shopgirls and exhausted clerks. But not here, for Madrid knew when to say No, and draw its shutters against the sun.

This, of course, was also the habit in other Spanish cities; but here it had reached a peak of particular genius. For Madrid at that time, if not today, was a city of a thousand exquisite taverns – water-cooled, barrel-lined, and cavernously spacious, cheap and affectionately run, in whose traditional shade the men, at least, spent a half of their waking time.

Stepping in from the torrid street, you met a band of cool air like fruit-peel pressed to your brow, and entered a cloistered grotto laden with the tang of shellfish, wet tiles, and wine-soaked wood. There was no waiting, no crowding; the place was yours; pot-boys took your orders with ringing cries; and men stood at their ease holding goblets of sherry, with plenty of time to drink them, while piled round the counters – succulently arranged in dishes or enthroned on great blocks of ice – lay banquets of sea-food : craggy oysters, crabs, calamares heaped in golden rings, fresh lobsters twitching on beds of palm-leaves, bowls of mussels, and feathery shrimps. Also on offer would be the little sizzling saucers of kidney or roasted sparrow, snails, fried squid, hot prawns in garlic, stewed pork or belly of lamb. Nobody drank without eating – it would have been thought uncivilized (and may have been one of the reasons why no one was drunk). But then this sea-food, after all, was some of the best in the world, land-locked Madrid's particular miracle, freshly gathered that morning from the far-away shores – the Mediterranean, Biscay, Atlantic – and rushed to the capital in special trains which pushed everything else into the sidings.

That's how I remember it: under the terra-cotta roofs, a proliferation of caves of ice. With carters, porters, watchmen, taxi-drivers, sleek dandies, and plump officials sipping their golden wines, fastidiously peeling a prawn, biting into the tart pink flesh of a lobster, tasting the living brine of half-forgotten seas, of half-remembered empires, while the surge of conversation continued like bubbling water under the framed pictures of bulls and heroes. It was a way of life evolved like a honey-comb and buried away from the burning sky; and perhaps no other city at that time had so successfully come to terms with this particular priority of pleasure.

But I think my most lasting impression was still the unhurried dignity and noblesse with which the Spaniard handled his drink. He never gulped, panicked, pleaded with the barman, or let himself be shouted into the street. Drink, for him, was one of the natural privileges of living, rather than the temporary suicide it so often is for others. But then it was lightly taxed here, and there were no licensing laws; and under such conditions one could take one's time.

I felt that Madrid was a city where I might make some money, so I went to the Town Hall to get the usual permission. The man examined my violin, hummed a few bars of *Il Travatore*, and said I should go to the Commissariat of Police. This was in another part of the city and got me nowhere, for I was passed on immediately to the Ministry of Agriculture. The officials were drowsily kind, rolled me cigarettes and asked me what I thought of Madrid, but although they seemed to approve of the idea of concerts in the streets, none of them could find the necessary form to permit it. But in the end it didn't matter; I was thanked for making the proper approaches and it was suggested I could go ahead without it.

So when the air cooled that evening, I went to the older part of the city, to the teeming cliffs above the Manzanares. There was scarcely any traffic; streets were intimate as courtyards, with lamplit arches smelling of wine and woodsmoke. And all were alive with that dense coming and going of a people too poor really to be going anywhere, content to walk up and down within sight of their neighbours, chewing carobs and sunflower seeds.

I melted easily enough into the evening crowds, playing alone but not entirely ignored. People walked from the shops to give me an apple or orange, and women threw paper-wrapped gifts from the balconies. 'Regard the young man. Find him a morsel, for Jesus' – and pennies and biscuits came scattering down.

Givers and receivers seemed to be equal here. It was a world of exchanges rather than charity. Stallholders swapped with their neighbours, or ate their own wares, and barmen poured out drinks for each other. Beggars were everywhere, sitting propped against walls, carefully inspecting one another's parcels, while around them ran rouged and painted children wearing their mothers' skirts and shoes.

This was a part of Madrid where I spent much of my time, especially those nights when nobody slept, sitting around till dawn on their little pavement chairs waiting for a breath of air from the Sierras. All was snug, drowsy, and closely wrapped, like life in some public bed. I remember the cries and conversations that rose and fell, looping from door to door:

'I buy ropes and iron, cottons and silks! I buy saucepans, nails, and keys!'

'Paco's no value. He's a mala lengua. He knows nothing but to sell old eggs.'

'She comes from Genoa – or her people did. He's from Burgos. He spies for the Guardia...'

'I have fritas, gambas, and pajaritos – fresh little mouthfuls, gentlemen...'

'Immaculada! – whore, where have you been all night? Whose mattress you been pressing then? ...'

There seemed no programme to life in these narrow alleys; nothing stopped and all hours were the same: always some mumbling old woman buying a half-litre of beans, a girl at a window, a child at the breast, some boy down a side-street silently torturing another, some family round a table eating...

And whenever I returned to my inn, no matter how late it might be, most of the carters would still be awake. The innkeeper would give me some coppers, or a glass of brandy, and suggest I play them a tune.

One night, I remember, a gentleman in a grey frock-coat came down from his room to listen, and stood close behind me, nodding and smiling to the music and sticking long silver pins through his throat.

Another night as I played, an old clock in the courtyard suddenly shuddered and struck fourteen.

'It's gone mad,' said the innkeeper. 'It hasn't struck for years.' And he went over and hit it with a bottle.

My bedroom was a cell without any windows, and had bedbugs as big as beetles. Lying down was to be ridden, racked, and eaten, to scratch and fight for breath. It was clear why everyone stayed awake in this city. Only in the streets and courtyards could one breathe at night, and the heat brought the beds alive.

Mornings, however, were miracles of renewal, well worth the short night's inferno. Then the sky was an infinity of bubble-blue, pure as a diamond seen through water, restoring to life the sleepless sufferers who emerged with faces shining like plates. Washed stones and wet dung scented the morning streets, together with the delicate tang of pine. Raised close to the sky, the city sparkled, as though among the first to receive its light. Indeed Madrid, the highest capital in Europe, was a crystal platform at this early hour, and the clarity of the air may have been the cause of a number of local obsessions – the people's concern for truth, their naked and pitiless mysticism, their fascination with pleasure and death. They were certainly lofty in their love of the city, putting it first among the many proverbs. 'From the provinces to Madrid – but from Madrid to the sky,' said one with ascending pride. Also: 'When I die, please God, let me go to Heaven, but have a little window to look back on Madrid.' Standing on its mile-high plateaux their city was considered to be the top rung of a ladder reaching just this side of paradise.

Mornings in the posada were the best time of the day, with

the walls dripping with watered flowers, I used to sit in the doorway, facing the street, while the girl Concha went to buy my breakfast; then when she returned she'd squat on the bench beside me and start pinning and curling her hair. Concha was a husky young widow from Aranjuez and spent most of the daytime idling about, waiting for the return of her boy-friend from the Asturias who brought her presents of jam and butter. In the meantime she was willing to do my marketing for me, so long as she could keep back a bit for herself.

She was in her ripe middle twenties, and I thought her mature and beautiful – though well out of reach of my years. Her heavy gold hair looked like a load of straw, and would have looked even better if she'd dyed it more often. She would ask me the usual questions. 'Why are you alone? Have you no wife or piccaneeky?' Sometimes she'd pour some fish-oil into the palms of my hands and get me to massage her hair with it. I'd be content to sit out the morning at this indolent task, while the carts rattled past in the street, and feel her leaning against me, heavy and silent, oblivious to the passing cries of the carters . . .

Finally, one morning, towards the end of my stay, I noticed her hot lazy eyes wandering over me. My clothes, she said, were without class or dignity and not proper for an Englishman. What I needed, at least, was a new pair of trousers, and she said she'd get some from a gentleman she knew. 'You will have them tonight, I promise you. Then you will be able to walk in the street with honour.'

That evening, in fact, I did well with the fiddle and spent the rest of the night in the bars. The hot still air sharpened the taste of the wine and sent me wandering from street to street, glad to be alone in this open city with all the benefits of no identity.

I began at the Calle Echegaray – a raffish little lane, half Goya, half Edwardian plush, with café-brothels full of painted mirrors, crippled minstrels, and lacquered girls. The narrow ditch-like alley was crowded with gypsies, watchmen, touts, and lechers, and with youths gazing aghast at the girls in the windows, without the money to buy them. Inside, the lucky ones – the paunchy bald clubmen, and spoiled señoritos spending their mothers' pin-money – had beer and prawns, a girl at each shoulder, a bootblack crouched at their feet, buying the fat court-life for a few pesetas in the midst of a clamour of crones and beggars.

I found a less brassy bar at the end of the street, one designed for quieter, more twilit drinking – but voluptuously furnished and decorated throughout with a Victorian amalgam of blood and sex. Varnished posters on the walls, the colour of old smoked salmon, announced: 'Toros en Valencia, 1911'; or showed Theda Bara-type beauties in black lace mantillas, roses pressed to their naked bosoms, sensuously posturing to a background of dying bullfighters, and choking bulls stretched on crimson sands.

In this bar the wine was poured from a great stone jar, and served by an old man who'd lost a leg in the bullring. He carried his grumbles and miseries like a guttering candle from one group of drinkers to another.

Someone mentioned Belmonte and Domingo Ortega, the two rival stars of the day.

'They are nothing,' he growled. 'Thieves and catch-pennies both. Don't speak of them to me. There are no men or bulls alive in Spain any more. Only pretty little boys with kittens.'

The wine was thick and strong, and I was still not used to it. The bar began to change dimensions. I was suddenly aware of the beauty of my fingernail, of people who addressed me, then disappeared.

A little man by my side was boasting in a sing-song voice of his home in the north of Spain. He was short, like a Welshman, with a sad chapel face, and was clearly enjoying his exile. He hated the void of Castille, the burnt-up desert; he came from a land of plenty. 'In the Asturias,' he was saying, while his companions giggled, 'there are three special kinds of green. The dark green of night, the clear green of water, and the pale fresh green of a corpse . . .'

Another man nearby suddenly spun round upon me and thrust his red butcher-face at mine.

'Long live Spain and Germany!' he said, raising his fist. 'Death to America! And long live Napoleon!'

'Napoleon's dead,' I said primly.

He gave me a cunning look.

'Oh, no; we believe he's alive.' He raised his fist again. 'But death to France too! – and if you're a Frenchman, excuse me...'

Then I was in another bar. It was quieter now. People were settling down to the middle hours of the night. Four men by the counter stood with their heads together, hands resting on one another's shoulders, intimate, hushed, middle-aged, and oblivious, taking turns to sing the verse of a song. Each one sang in a distant, ghostly falsetto, while the rest bent their heads to the words, and their long jowled faces, intent and listening, were creased in silent pleasure. Such a group, heads joined in an English pub, would have been known to be swapping dirty jokes; and the songs these men were singing were also sex-jokes in a way, but polished by a thousand anonymous poets – stinging rhymes about passion, the decay of powers, seduction, defeat, and death.

I ended that night, my last in Madrid, with a visit to the Bar Chicote – not the prophylactic night-spot it later became for tourists, but a place of unassumingly local indulgence. More like a private room than a public tavern, it had an atmosphere of exhausted eroticism, and the girls sat quietly in the shadows, subdued but glowing, like daughters waiting to run away from home.

The clients included a few priestly old men and a handful of worn-out dandies, all scrupulously dressed and sprawled at their drinks as if the furniture had been fitted round them. On a stool in one corner a foxlike guitarist whistled through his teeth as he played, and there was a diminutive singer, anxious and hungry, who gave sudden little yelping laughs, and who sat, when not singing, with his lips at the ready, folded back round his shining gums.

Having a few pesetas left, I found a table, and soon there was a girl beside me, whispering wooingly in broken English, full of instant charm and lies. I remember the small gypsy face, fine as

an Indian dancer's, and the chaste white buttoned-up blouse.
She told me she had a gentleman-friend in America who sent
her a hundred dollars a month. 'But I am a bad girl – Lowry –
much too bad.' She stroked my arm with her purple fingers.
'Because how romantic I am. How just poetic. I am for nothing
but the heart, you know.' She had summed me up quickly. 'I
love England, Lowry. I love Cardiff and Hartlepool. I would go
with you anywhere.' She ordered more drinks, her head a few
inches from mine, energy lighting her face like water. Whispering across her glass: 'My friend in America, he has four, five
children. He sends me their photographs. He won't come back.
How just romantic I am. Lowry, you take me with you. I
wouldn't be bad against you . . .'

Another drink, and I was imagining this girl barefooted,
walking beside me, rolled in my blanket at night. But suddenly
there was a racket at the door, followed by one of those
theatrical entrances – a minor bullfighter with his court of
gypsies. Shouts, embraces, a busy stir at the bar, a yelp of song
from the awakened singer. And I was alone again, watching
the girl's empty glass rolling sideways across the table.

I walked back through the streets with a rocking head, thinking simple ironic thoughts. It was long past midnight, almost
dawn, and for once Madrid seemed deserted. The posada was
closed, but the door opened to my shoulder and cats darted
across the yard like lizards.

As I stumbled upstairs a hand touched mine in the darkness
and drew me into a jumbled moonlit room. 'I've got your
clothes,' said Concha. She stood close against me, holding my
shoulder-blades, and I could smell her peppery flesh. 'Man,' she
whispered. I swayed on my feet, full of hazy, unthinking
dumbness. Somewhere in the room a child called 'Mama', and
the woman paused to give it a spoonful of jam. Then she took
off my boots and helped me to bed. Before she joined me she
made the sign of the cross.

# 7. Toledo

Two days later I walked into Toledo, about forty miles to the south, and there the Castilian sun caught up with me at last and struck me down with a twenty-four-hour fever.

I'd found a brilliant white inn just inside the city gate, so dazzling it seemed to be carved from salt, but the bruising impact it made on the eyes soon warned me that something was wrong.

I remember climbing into the town, hugging the narrow shadows and accompanied by rainbow hallucinations, then staggering into a wineshop for a glass of water and dropping unconscious on the floor. When I recovered, I remembered two men carrying me back to the inn and laying me down by a water-trough. Racked with icy heat, I pressed my face to the stone, grateful for the smell of its damp green mould, and dimly aware of the crackle of female voices discussing my poor condition.

They sat in a circle around me, a group of thin old women, pyramids of black against the shimmering walls, carefully keeping their distance but watching me closely with a mixture of concern and exasperation. 'Ay! ... It's his head ... He walks without a hat ... The foolish ... The sad young man ...' Meanwhile I was left alone to sweat and sleep, and not even the dogs approached me.

I was still lying out there in the middle of the night, still lying where the men had put me. I could feel the stone of the water-trough against my cheek, and there was a cold white moon overhead. Everybody else was asleep, and the courtyard was empty, but someone had covered me with a sack.

By noon next day the fever suddenly went, leaving me purged and ravenously hungry. The women were back on their chairs, knees spread, hands folded, grouped silently around the walls. Seeing me sit up, one of them brought me some food and told me not to be such a fool in future. The others nodded in chorus, pointing their fingers at the sun and shrinking away in postures of dread. 'Bad! bad!' they cried, drawing their scarves across their faces till only their eyes and knuckles were showing.

That evening I was back on the job, playing to the open-air cafés in the Plaza de Zocodover – a sloping square of uneven cobbles which was the town's main centre. No traffic, no radios – only the sun-down crowds quietly sitting and watching each other, the waiters mostly idle or flicking at flies with slow caressive movements.

I'd not been there long when a special party arrived and

made their way to a nearby table – a curiously striking group and immediately noticeable in the ponderous summer twilight. There were four of them: a woman in dazzling white, a tall man wearing a broad black hat, a jaunty young girl with a rose in her hair, followed by a pretty lacy child.

They were clearly not Spanish, yet they had a Spanish air. I thought they might possibly have been Portuguese. The man sat at the table with a distinguished stoop, while his companions arranged themselves gracefully beside him, spreading their shawls on the chairs and beaming round the darkening square as though in a box at the opera. I finished my last tune and began to take a collection, which brought me at last to their table. The woman asked me in French if I was German, and I replied in Spanish that I was English. 'Ah,' she smiled. 'And so am I.' And she invited me to join them.

The man shifted and coughed. He had a long scorched face and the eyes of a burnt-out eagle. He offered me a strong but shaky hand. 'Roy Campbell,' he said. 'South African poet. Er – reasonably well known in your country.'

His voice was musically hoarse, yet broken and interrupted as though being transmitted on faulty wires, and it seemed to quaver between bursts of sudden belligerence and the most humble of hesitations.

In a series of stuttering phrases he rapidly let it be known that he hated England, that all his friends were English, that English literature was an unburied corpse, that he was in Spain because England had no manhood any more; and was I broke and could he help me at all?

The diatribe was short, all over in a moment, like a quick shuffling of totem-masks. Then with affectionate dignity he introduced his companions, inclining his long broad back to each. Mary, his wife, his small daughter Anna, and their Catalan friend, Amelia.

It was the poet's saint's-day, and the party had dressed in his honour and were drinking his health in fizzy pop. Campbell himself drank wine in long shuddering gasps, and suggested I do the same. I was more than satisfied by this encounter, which had come so unexpectedly out of the evening, pleased to have arrived on foot in this foreign city in time to be elected to this poet's table. All things were as they should be – the artist in exile, generous and defiant in mood, his red eyes glittering like broken glass as the phrases came stumbling forth. Still tense and light-headed from my recent fever, I felt the glory of the Word around me, and accepted the stature of the man without surprise, imagining all poets to be made like this.

Then Mary Campbell inquired how long I'd been in Toledo, and whether I was on my own. 'D'you like rissotto?' she asked, and said she was sure there was more than enough if I cared to go home with them for supper.

The Campbells had rented a house under the wall of the Cathedral, in Cardinal Cisneros – a typically bare-fronted place with an elegant patio inside surrounded by a gallery of little rooms.

Supper was served in the patio under the open sky, with several bottles of local wine, and I found myself sitting down to a well-laid table for the first time in almost two months. The young girls were excited and ready to make the most of the feast-day, and they dressed up as gypsies to entertain us – dancing and weaving among the old stone pillars to the fluttering light of candles. Little Anna, who was about five years old, had blue eyes and thick black hair, and she danced like a firefly, floating over the flagstones with a precocious, iridescent skill.

Afterwards, they changed again and acted out a shrill Spanish play – aided by the housemaid dressed up as a hag. The epic was long, in dialect, and devoted to the complications of jealousy, during which Roy and I fell asleep.

When the girls had gone to bed, we woke up again and talked until early morning. Roy also read a few poems in his thick trembling voice, monotonous, yet curiously moving, and nothing could have suited me better at that hour, and at that place and time of my life. I was young, full of wine, and in love with poetry, and was hearing it now from the poet's mouth. It came out in agony, bruised yet alive, and each line seemed to shake his body. He read some of his shorter poems. 'Horses on the Camargue', 'The Sisters', 'Choosing a Mast', and the words seemed to flare at the nostrils, whinny and thunder, and rise like steam in the air.

Half-dazed with sleep, I felt my eyelids falling, printed with succulent images : sisters called to their horses, naked in the dark, and met them with silken thighs; a rich Zulu nipple plugged the mouth of a child; mares went rolling beneath the hooves of stallions . . . What had I read till then? – cartloads of Augustan whimsy; this, I felt, was the stuff for me.

Presently he finished reading and began to talk and gossip, swaying to and fro in his chair. He spoke of his friends and enemies, pinning scandals to most of them, boasting of quarrels, feuds, and fights. The scene, as he described it, was of a six-foot South African striding contemptuously among the pygmies. Famous names were set up to be torn apart, somewhat confusing to me at the time – Eliot, A. E. Coppard, Wyndham Lewis, Marie Corelli, Jacob Epstein, T. E. Lawrence, the Sitwells. 'Osbert Sitwell? – knocked him down in – ah – Charlotte Street. Him and his coronet . . . Didn't like Coppard – I kicked his ass. Mary will tell you. That's the truth now, isn't it?'

Mary sat listening and saying nothing, cool and white in her dress. In fact it was T. E. Lawrence, he admitted, who had helped to place him as a poet, bringing his first book to the critics' attention. He was one of the few of his friends for whom he had a good word that night – apart from Augustus John.

The Campbells had first met John, Roy told me, before they were married, when they were living in the south of France, at Martigues – a village on a lagoon near the mouth of the Rhône, full of bad water and drink-crazed fishermen. John had adopted the lovers, as well he might, for they must have been an unusually handsome pair; and had helped, in due course, to arrange their wedding, which took place in the wilderness of the Camargue. It had been a 'gypsy' affair, designed like an early John canvas, with caravans, campfires, ceremonial mixings of blood, heavy drinking, and trials of strength, reaching its climax when the couple mounted a couple of horses and galloped away across the midnight plain. (This was a typical Roy fantasy : in fact he met Mary in London, married her soon after, and they spent their honeymoon with the Johns in Dorset. True, there had been a loud 'gypsy' party – held in a pub near Parkstone – and later indeed they had gone to live in Martigues.)

But John would have picked out the poet and his black-haired girl anywhere as though he himself had created them – Mary, with her violet-eyed Celtic beauty, and Roy the deep-browed giant wildly bearded like a lustier Yeats. This was only a few years back, but trembling Roy, as he talked, became again the hero of Martigues, towering in his strength above the small blue fishermen, their brawling champion at arms, out-sailing, out-rowing, out-drinking them – then spending inexhaustible nights of love.

'We never grew tired of it, did we, girl? We must have broken half the beds in the town.'

'Roy – please,' his wife murmured, touching her lavender lips. 'I'm sure he doesn't want to hear all that.'

They asked me to stay the night, and I slept in a little room off the patio, on a mattress propped up by books. Other books lay scattered across the floor, together with sheaves of unfinished poems. I remember peering at one of them, a single line in the candlelight – something about storm-hornets snoring in the wind . . .

Nobody stirred the next morning, except the carolling housemaid, who brought me some breakfast and took my shirt to wash. I got up and wandered about the deserted patio, where I found a note suggesting I stay on if I wished; so I went back to the inn, collected my bags from the old ladies, and returned gratefully to the book-filled room. Roy reappeared at lunch, still tousled with sleep, and talked brokenly throughout the meal, shaking about him as he ate tattered plumes of nerves but slowly regaining his claims to glory.

He'd sailed whalers, swum Hellesponts, broken horses on the Camargues, fought bulls, and caught sharks barehanded. He'd stirred up two hemispheres, as well as the olive-belt between, and restored blood and muscle to poetry. His voice, growing hoarser as though blown through a shell, continued to boom like an ancient mariner's, not so much determined, I felt, to convince me of the truth of these legends as hoping to suggest that this was how a man should live.

In fact, there was something curiously inoffensive about his boasting, it was warm-hearted and even childlike, breathless, confidential, as though he wished you to share in the secret – that anyone on earth could have done such things if only they'd been lucky like him.

After lunch, and the long tidal flow of wine, Roy staggered off to have another sleep. But Mary and I sat on through the hot afternoon while she instructed me about religion. It was only then that I noticed the crucifixes in the house, decorated with knots of jasmine, and recalled where the Campbells had chosen to live, in this street pressed close to the walls of the Cathedral, wrapped in its mantle of bells and incense. I was a heretic, of course, and opinionated; jaunty with my lack of belief. But Mary Campbell, soft-voiced and shining-eyed, reproved me with gentle calm. And in her, for the first time, I saw the banked-up voluptuousness of a young and beautiful convert, holding to this single passion in which all hungers were answered and all doubts quietly put away. Here, romantic love was kept on ice, sealed by an unfaltering spiritual flame, and accompanied by a vocabulary of torment, physical denial and ecstacy which promised an eternity of sensuous reward.

It may also have been the first, and most dangerous, time – as I sat with the poet's wife through that hushed afternoon, watching her finger her beads in the airless shade – that I felt the pull of that seductive faith.

But I argued against it – at that age I wanted action, not the devout pause before some deferred consummation; I wanted the excitement of doubt, the satisfaction of mortality, the freedom to make love here and now on earth. Beautiful Mary would have none of it; she sat among her pin-up ikons, smiling quietly, unshakably contained. 'Don't you see?' she kept saying (we were damned if we didn't). 'You can't *imagine* the utter peace . . .'

I stayed with the Campbells for about a week, and was treated with a matter-of-fact kindness which surprised and charmed me. I'd arrived from nowhere, but nobody bothered me with questions; I was simply accepted and given the run of the house.

During most of the daylight hours Roy lay low and slept, appearing at nightfall like some ruffled sea-bird, leaning against a pillar with his arms stretched wide as though drying his salt-wet wings. One saw him gathering his wits in great gulps of breath, after which he would be ready for anything.

Mary and little Anna lived in an intimate calm of their own, quietly busy with their spiritual chores, and could be seen in the morning going off to Mass, veiled and modest as shadows, and so native in appearance that when I met them in the street I often forgot and addressed them in Spanish. When they returned from their devotions they would come back transformed, light-footed and chirpy with gossip, their early silence now swept away, and their eyes sparkling, as though they'd been to a party.

One evening, to keep my hand in, I played for an hour in the streets and made over seven pesetas, in copper. I carried it back to the house and poured it out on the table, to the delight of the astonished girls. We bought a few litres of wine and went up on to the roof, where there was a terrace with a view of the city. It was still light, and the humped little red-tiled houses, scaled and patchy, clustered around us like crabs.

We ate supper and drank, and as the evening darkened, Roy coughed and began to sing, croaking the corny laments and border ballads that were near to his expatriate heart. His voice was blurred as usual, and rough as a sailor's, yet deeply charged with feeling; more than that, he sang with a poet's care, renewing the worn, familiar words. 'Scots Wa Hae', 'The Bonnie Earl of Murray', sounded as if they'd just been written – with the blood of the slain still wet. To me, until then, they'd just been songs of the schoolroom, now I heard them fresh and bitter, while Roy sat with hunched shoulders, rocking backwards and forwards, often at the point of tears.

Suddenly the maid, from somewhere down in the house, hearing his singing, started up too – not a brash interruption, but like a night-bird answering to the husky call of another. Sad Castillian airs, harsh but haunting, came floating up the well of the stairs. Each new song from Roy would call up another from the girl, rising like bubbles of grief in the darkness, not clashing with his but hovering round the edges, offering a compassionate echo.

Later, the night grew cold, and we huddled under furs and blankets, talking till nearly dawn. Summer lightning and shooting stars lit up the Toledo sky with little soundless conflagrations, flickering across the Cathedral and over the faces of the poet and his wife like ripples of phosphorescence.

Roy drank four and a half litres of wine a day, he said – thin, sharp stuff, lobster pink in colour, and one of the consolations of living in Toledo. Another, for him, was the paintings of El Greco, which were stacked all over the town. 'Never seen him? You must. Bloody marvellous, boy. Wake me up tomorrow, and I'll take you round.'

We began by going to the Museo de San Vicente, to see the 'Annunciation'. Campbell stood quietly before it, bare-headed, slightly bowed, his eyes blinking beneath their sun-bleached lashes; and I first saw the canvas as it were through him, by his physical stance and silence. Then muttering, without jargon, but with a kind of groping reverence, he explained what the painting meant to him. 'A bloody miracle, that hand. And look at that light in the sky. Pure Toledo – only he was the first bugger to see it.'

Then we went higher up the town to El Greco's house – still preserved in its sloping garden; a beautiful, shaggy, intimate little villa, full of dead flowers and idiot guides. Inside were the paintings : colours I'd never seen before, weeping purples, lime greens, bitter yellows; the long skulls of the saints and their sunken eyelids, eyes coated with ecstatic denials, limbs and faces drawn upwards like spires ascending, robes flickering like tapered flames – compared with the robust flesh-painting I'd seen in Madrid, these seemed to be reduced to the fevered bone.

El Greco exhausted us both. It was torrid noon, so we spent the rest of the day in the bars. Roy had started out that morn-

ing with a trembling melancholy, walking unsteadily, stuttering with weakness. As we drank, he grew stronger, taller,
happy, embracing and singing, full of intimate asides. 'Marvellous girl, that Mary. Wonderful wife. She keeps her thoughts to
herself. She's got more genuine saintliness in her little finger
than the whole of this god-damn town.'

But it was clear that he was known with affection in Toledo
– at least, by the men in the bars. Leathery hands reached up to
lean on his shoulders, processions of dwarfs brought him
tumblers of wine. Heads were raised, slightly cocked, to hear
what he had to say. Meanwhile he introduced me to everyone.

'A champion, this boy. Walked all the way from Vigo. He
walks a thousand miles a week. It's true, by God...' Dwarfs
brought me wine, too. Roy kept repeating : 'The funny thing is
– he's English.'

During the long afternoon, amidst waves of euphoria, Roy
would also be visited by brief moments of panic. He'd suddenly
say it was midnight, and that he'd got to go to Mass, and start
searching his pockets for a collar and tie. The shepherds would
take him by the arm, lead him out into the street, and show
him the position of the sun – at which he would blink and nod,
say 'Bless my soul', and return relieved to his drinking.

In the evening we drank brandy. I don't know where we
were, but we were sitting on barrels in a kind of cave. The
brandy was smooth and warm, straight from the cask, and had
a flavour of muscatels. Roy talked about his career and was
surprised at it. He spoke of his poetry with humility. Edith
Sitwell had written to a paper to say he would make a likely
Poet Laureate, and this had amused him and also helped his
sales. He told me how much money he'd been paid by various
publishers for books he would never write. This amused him
too. And so did his autobiography, *Broken Record*, which he'd
recently published and which he said was largely a spoof to
confuse his enemies.

That night, mixing drinks, he also mixed his emotions,
swinging between love and hatred – singing, cursing, offering to
lend me money, shaking with pleasure at some success of his
youth, praising God, the Virgin Mary, and Mary his wife, and

punching out satirical couplets. He loved the Afrikaans language and described its primitive vigour. He hated Amelia for going to Mass dressed like a whore. He hated socialism, dog-lovers, and English dons. He loved fighting, heroism, and pain.

Yet for all his verbal arrogance, chest-beating, and boasting, I found him a curiously gentle companion. 'Look, I must get you some books. You don't mind, do you? And I've got a razor you can have...' His manner to those he accepted was warm, modest, and at times almost haltingly apologetic, and the locals we drank with that night treated him not as a joke foreigner to be fleeced, but as a poet and man of their own.

I spent my last morning at the Campbells' shaking the brandy fumes from my head and enjoying the final luxuries of the house. The maid scrubbed and sang. Mary carried roses to the church. Little Anna ran about watering the flower pots. Roy slept, while Amelia sat sewing nearby and darting angry glances at his door.

At midday there was a meal of stuffed marrow and salad, accompanied by bottles of Málaga wine. I was packed and ready. 'Don't go in the heat,' they said. Anna said, 'You don't have to go at all.' So I lingered through the afternoon in another metaphysical exercise with Mary, ending with tea and sugared cakes. Snatches of England – flowered china and silver teaspoons – haunted the heavy Spanish air.

Roy woke up in time to take me down to the bridge, by which I would cross the gorge of the Tagus. Here we said good-bye. 'Write if you get short of money,' he said, looking down at me like some puzzled and anxious parent. 'Come back if you want to. Er – we might have gone to Mexico – but we'll always be glad to see you...' He coughed and shook hands. Crossing the bridge I looked back and saw him still standing in the road, legs astride, shoulders hunched, head drooping. He raised his wide-brimmed hat and held it high for a moment, then turned and stumbled back into the town.

# 8. To the Sea

Now it was the end of September and I'd reached the sea, having taken almost three months to come down through Spain. Cádiz, from a distance, was a city of sharp incandescence, a scribble of white on a sheet of blue glass, lying curved on the bay like a scimitar and sparkling with African light.

In fact it was a shut-in city, a kind of Levantine ghetto almost entirely surrounded by sea – a heap of squat cubist hovels enclosed by medieval ramparts and joined to the mainland by a dirty thread of sand.

I lived in an evil old posada whose galleries were packed with sailors, beggars, and pimps; and there was little to do all day except sit round in the dust while the scorching winds blew in from the Atlantic.

The police said it was forbidden to play music in the streets for money, so sometimes I played for nothing. Or I went round the cafés with a blind brother and sister who helped out my fiddle with a couple of goat-skin drums. When we were lucky we were rewarded with a few scraps of food, otherwise we played to amuse ourselves, or simply sat round talking, drinking from cracked tin cups, and eating prawns out of screws of paper.

I seemed to meet no one in Cádiz except the blind and the crippled, the diseased, the deaf and dumb, whose condition was so hopeless they scarcely bothered to complain but treated it all as a twisted joke. They told me tittering tales of others even more wretched than themselves – the homeless who lived in the Arab drains, who lay down at night among rats and excrement and were washed out to sea twice a year by the floods. They told me of families who scraped the tavern floors for shellfish and took it home to boil for soup, and of others who lived by trapping cats and dogs and roasting them on fires of driftwood. They even took me one night to a tenement near the cathedral and pointed out a howling man on the rooftop, who was pretending to be a ghost in order to terrorize the landlord and thereby reduce the rents.

I'd been travelling through Spain in a romantic haze, but as I came south the taste grew more bitter. Cádiz at that time was nothing but a rotting hulk on the edge of a disease-ridden tropic sea; its people dismayed, half-mad, consoled only by vicious humour, prisoners rather than citizens.

Since I left the Campbells in Toledo I'd been almost a month on the road; a month of vintage September weather; travelling in easy stages through autumnal landscapes which seemed to be moistly wrapped in fruit-skins. I'd been glad to be back on

my solitary marches, edging mindlessly from village to town,
sleeping in thickets, in oases of rushes, under tall reeds, to the
smell of water. South of Toledo there was green country still
– green trees against brick-red earth, trees so intense they
seemed to throw green shade and turn the dust around them to
grass.

There were purple evenings, juicy as grapes, the thin moon
cutting a cloud like a knife; and dawns of quick sudden
thunder when I'd wake in the dark to splashes of rain pouring
from cracks of lightning, then walk on to a village to sit cold
and alone, waiting for it to wake and sell me some bread,
watching the grey light lifting, a man opening a stable, the first
girls coming to the square for water.

Out in the open country it grew dark early, and then there
was nothing to do but sleep. As the sun went down, I'd turn
into a field and curl up like a roosting bird, then wake in the
morning soaked with dew, before the first farmer or the sun
was up, and take to the road to get warm, through a smell of
damp herbs, with the bent dawn moon still shining.

In the valley of the Guadiana I saw herds of black bulls
grazing in fields of orange dust, and square white farms, like
desert strongholds, protected by packs of savage dogs. Somewhere here, in a barn, under a roof crusted with swallows'
nests, a mother and daughter cooked me a supper of eggs,
while a horse watched me eating, chickens walked on the
table, and an old man in the hay lay dying.

Then as I approached Valdepeñas a carter offered me a lift,
exclaiming that no stranger should walk while he rode, and
proudly answered my gift of a cigarette by giving me in ex-
change a miniature cucumber. On our way to the town we
stopped at a village fair and watched the performance of an
open-air circus, which consisted of a monkey, a camel, an
Arab, a snake, and two painted little boys with trumpets.

Valdepeñas was a surprise: a small graceful town surrounded
by rich vineyards and prosperous villas – a pocket of good fortune which seemed to produce without effort some of the most
genial wines in Spain. The town had an air of privileged well-

being, like an oil-well in a desert of hardship; the old men and children had extra flesh on their bones, and even the dogs seemed to shine with fat.

It was also a friendly town, where people welcomed my violin and encouraged me to play as though I'd come to a wedding, drawing back their shutters, leaning over their balconies, and rewarding me with food and money. I remember playing in the evenings to houses of blue and white, while women approached me with cups of wine, and the pork-fattened shopkeepers broke off from kissing their children to bring me parcels of ham and olives.

Then one night, as I was having my supper in the square, three young men invited me to a brothel. They addressed me as 'Maestro', and introduced themselves formally: Antonio, Amistad, and Julio. I would be doing them a bounty, they said, and led me off through the town, waving their arms and making spry little dances.

Somewhere out in the suburbs we came to an old dark house, windowless, with a heavy door. The boys kicked it delicately with their pointed shoes and made low-pitched animal cries. Their teeth shone as they waited, and heat seemed to rise from the ground. The house appeared to be empty. Then the door was opened at last by a girl in a dressing-gown, sleepily eating chips.

'Guapos,' she said, in a warm flat voice, holding her arm across the doorway.

'We've brought music,' said Julio. 'Let us in, Consuelito.'

'Why not?' yawned the girl, and we entered.

Inside was a bare little patio roofed by a trellis of vines and hung with a string of coloured light-bulbs. 'We are always expected, you understand,' said Julio. 'But they will be diverted if you play a little.'

A half-dressed young girl sat at the foot of the stairs polishing her toenails with a hairbrush. Two others were sprawled at a table poring over the pages of a comic. The patio wore an air of low-lit ennui.

Consuelito bolted the door, took another mouthful of chips, then threw back her head and shrieked 'Grandpa!'; at which a giggling old greybeard trotted immediately from the kitchen bearing a trayful of wine and food.

He gave us a frisky welcome, fussily filling our glasses, beating off the flies as if they were ravens, calling us masters, dukes, princes, kings, and commanding his granddaughters to stiffen their backs.

When we were comfortably settled, the old man took the violin from my hands and returned it with a little bow. 'Enchant us,' he said, and slipped me some money. The girls rose slowly to their feet and joined us.

I remember the whoosh of the wine going through my limbs, the throbbing and familiar fires, as I sat with my feet across the table scraping out waltzes and pasodobles. Julio beat time with a couple of spoons, Antonio tapped his teeth with a knife, while Amistad, already as pink as a prawn, sang away in a sickly tenor.

Business steadily grew brisker as the night advanced; the front door was increasingly kicked; there were whispers, shadowy figures stumbling their way upstairs, the sounds of boots and bare feet overhead. Grandpa found an accordion, which he gave to Antonio, and together we kept up our wheezy concert. Meanwhile the beaming old man half-drowned us with wine and said we were an honour to the house.

During short intervals of quiet the girls rejoined us, yawning and re-settling their hair, nibbling our food and chattering together in voices that were hoarse and furry with sleep. They were sturdy girls, with ruddy hands and faces, and strong absent-minded bodied, and judging from their appearance one might have thought they earned their bread in the fields rather than in this breathless and shuttered house. Two were sisters, the other two cousins, and they were all in their early teens. We seemed to be the youngest visitors they had that night, most of the others being middle-aged farmers.

The four girls and Grandpa made up an intimate establishment which for a brothel appeared strangely muted. I'd expected noise, livid flesh, drunken voices, obscenities, or a kind of hang-dog, ravenous shame. Instead there was this casual atmosphere of neighbourly visiting, hosted by these vague and sleepy girls; subdued talk, a little music, an air of domestic eroticism, with unhurried comings and goings.

At last there was silence in the house, and a gleam of dawn in the patio. I sat fuddled with wine in my chair. The boys were asleep at the table, and Grandpa lay asleep on the floor, curled up like a wrinkled child. The youngest of the cotton-wrapped girls came and shook him by the arm. 'Grandpa, the farmers have gone,' she said. The old man woke up, whispered something in her ear, winked at me, and went to sleep again.

The girl shrugged, yawned, and came across to my table. I felt her lean soft and drowsily against me. She put a long brown finger to the neck of my shirt and drew it slowly down my body. Little shocks ran through me, see-saw surges of feeling, warm vaultings of sleepy comfort. The girl's wandering finger, tipped with precocious cunning, seemed the only thing left alive in the world, and moved absently about me, loosening knots in my flesh, then tying them up again.

A few days later, in a village south of Valdepeñas, I ran into Romero, a young tramp like myself, who was carrying his goods wrapped in a bundle of sailcloth and explained that he was on the road for his health. When he heard what I was doing he threw up his arms and said that was just the thing. He would go with me anywhere, he said, collect the money when I played, scrounge me food, and show me the country.

As I'd been alone for some time it seemed a good idea, so we left the village together – Romero prancing beside me, talking of ways to make money, boasting of his spectacular skill as a cook, of the various tricks he knew of enticing fowls from farmers, and of begging from nuns in convents. He was a handsome young man, witty and unscrupulous, and I felt he had some useful things to teach me. We camped the first night on a threshing floor – a circle of flagstones in the middle of a field – and lay side by side under a single blanket watching the large red sun go down. I still remember the moment: the sun huge on the horizon and the silhouette of a horseman passing slowly across it, with Romero whispering and rolling me cigarettes, and his warmth as the evening cooled.

My pleasure in his company lasted about three days, then soured and diminished quickly. No longer could I imagine myself prince of the road, the lone ranger my fancy preferred. I'd developed an ingrowing taste for the vanity of solitude, and Romero's presence cut into this sharply. Besides, he was sluggish and lazy, was always whining for vino and complaining about his feet. Certainly he detested walking, and after a mile or so would throw himself down and kick like a baby; so after lunch one day, while he was sleeping by the roadside, I put some money in his shoe and left him.

It was an extraordinary relief to be on my own again, and I made for the hills as fast as I could. But he must have awoken soon after, for presently I heard a distant shout, and there he was, coming in furious pursuit. Throughout the rest of the day I caught glimpses of him in the distance, a small toiling figure, head down and determined, scurrying indignantly along in the dust. Feeling both guilty and hunted, I quickened my pace, and gradually he fell away. There was one last cry, as from an abandoned wife, and I never saw him again.

Then I came to the Sierra Morena – one more of those east–west ramparts which go ranging across Spain and divide its people into separate races. Behind me was Old Castile and the Gothic north; beyond, the Sierra the spiced blur of Andalusia.

A peasant stopped me in the foothills (a twinge of agony on his face at the sight of my road-worn feet) and piled my bags on his mule, gave me a stick, and said he would show me the way up the mountain. We climbed for three hours, up a rope-ladder of goat tracks which led up through a wilderness of rocks – a great jumble of boulders, large as houses, which seemed to have been thrown about by giants. The mule and I stumbled, but my guide climbed ahead of us, light-footed, never looking back. Sometimes he nodded towards the crags and made a reference to bandits. Occasionally we saw a goat-herd sitting brown and alone.

At last we pushed through the peaks and came to a misty plateau with a chill breeze blowing across it. Here was my companion's village – a huddle of rough-stone hovels, primitively rounded and tufted with dripping moss. A few diseased-looking sheep, with ribs like radiators, wandered in and out of the houses.

When they heard us coming the villagers gathered in the mist and waited for my companion to explain who I was. After he'd done this briefly, as best he could, they gave me a meal of bread and curds. Then, with a muted apology, my guide took the violin from its bag and handed it to me delicately, like a new-born lamb. I was now used to this reception – the ritual gift of food, followed by the offered instrument and the expectant silence.

I remember the villagers as they listened, blankets held to their throats, dribbles of damp lying along their eyebrows. I felt I could have been with some lost tribal remnant of seventeenth-century Scotland, during one of their pauses between famine and massacre – the children standing barefooted in puddles of dew, old women wrapped in their rancid sheepskins, and the short shaggy men whose squinting faces seemed stuck between a smile and a snarl.

When I'd finished playing, they filled my bottle with wine and stuffed some stone-hard cheese in my pocket. Then we said good-bye, and I left them standing on the ridge of the plateau like a cluster of wind-bent thorn bushes.

South of the Sierra the mists rolled away, and I met a new kind of heat, brutal and hard, carrying the smell of another continent. As I came down the mountain this heat piled up, pushing against me with blasts of sand, so that I walked half-blind, my tongue dry as a carob bean, obsessed once again by thirst. These were ominous days of nerve-bending sirocco, with peasants wrapped up to the eyes, during which I was savagely bitten by a demented dog with eyes like yellow gas. The southern slopes of the Sierras were flaking in the wind, parched as a rusty furnace, but far down in the valley, running in slow green coils, I could see at last the tree-lined Guadalquivir. Viewed from the blistered heights it was a mirage-river, which I remember putting into a short rough poem:

Rinsed sweat from the bare Sierras
courses a curled furrow in the dust

a sun-dazed wanderer
staggering to the sea ...

When I reached the river at sundown I found it red, not green – shallow red water running between banks of red earth under a heavy scarlet sky, with flocks of red goats coming down to drink in clouds of vermilion dust. Naked boys, with bodies like copper pennies, splashed about in the shining mud, and all around was the rich and water-fed valley – shimmering eucalyptus, gardens of figs and peaches, orchards of plums fringed by tropical cacti, with loads of fat blackberries along the side of the road which I picked and ate for supper.

Entering the province of Andalusia through fields of ripening melons, I saw the first signs of the southern people : men in tall Cordobese hats, blue shirts, scarlet waistbands, and girls with smouldering Arab faces. Villages had Moorish names – Andújar, Pedro Abad – and an air of proud though listless anarchy. In the main square of one, fully exposed to the populace, I saw two prisoners in an iron cage, puffing cheerily at cigarettes, blowing smoke through the bars, and shouting obscenities at the passers-by.

At this point on the road I might have continued south to Granada, which was only two or three days away. Instead I turned west and followed the Guadalquivir, which added several months to my journey, and took me to the sea the roundabout way and affected everything that was later to happen to me.

Ever since childhood I'd imagined myself walking down a white dusty road through groves of orange trees to a city called Seville. This fantasy may have been induced by the Cotswold damp, or by something my mother had told me, but it was one of several such clichés which had brought me to Spain, and now as I approached the city on this autumn morning it was as though I was simply following some old direction.

In fact there was no white road, not even a gold-clustered orange tree, but Seville itself was dazzling – a creamy crustation of flower-banked houses fanning out from each bank of the river. The Moorish occupation had bequeathed the affection for water around which so many of even the poorest dwellings were built – a thousand miniature patios set with inexhaustible fountains which fell trickling upon ferns and leaves, each a nest of green repeated in endless variations around this theme of domestic oasis. Here the rippling of water replaced the coal-fire of the north as a symbol of home and comfort, while its whispering presence, seen through grilles and doorways, gave an impression of perpetual afternoon, each house turning its back on the blazing street outside to lie coiled around its moss-cool centre.

Seville was no paradise, even so. There was the customary squalor behind it – children and beggars sleeping out in the gutters under a coating of disease and filth. By day their condition seemed somewhat less intolerable, and they presented a jaunty face to the world. All were part of the city – the adored Seville – to which even the beggars claimed pride of belonging, and where ragged little girls would raise their thin brown arms and dance rapturously at the least excuse. It was a city of traditional alegria, where gaiety was almost a civic duty, something which rich and poor wore with arrogant finesse simply because the rest of Spain expected it. Like the Viennese, the Sevillanas lived under this burden of legend, and were forced into carefree excesses, compelled to flounce and swagger as the embodiment of Andalusia in spite of frequent attacks of liverish exhaustion.

I lived in Seville on fruit and dried fish, and slept at night in a yard in Triana – that ramshackle barrio on the north bank of the river which was once a gypsy ghetto. In my day it still had a seedy vigour, full of tile-makers and free-range poultry, of medieval stables bursting with panniered donkeys, squabbling wives and cooking pots. Stately cockerels with brilliant combs and feathers strutted like Aztecs about the rooftops, while from my yard I could hear the incessant throb of guitars being practised in shuttered rooms.

Seville in the morning was white and gold, the gold-lit river reflecting the Toro de Oro, with flashes of sun striking the Giralda Tower and the spires of the prostrate cathedral. The interior of the cathedral was a bronze half-light, a huge cavern of private penance, with an occasional old woman hobbling about on her knees, mumbling a string of prayers, or some transfixed girl standing in a posture of agony, arms stretched before the bleeding Christ.

At the morning market I bought cactus fruit, dripping with juice and shot full of seeds, sold by a garrulous old man who entertained his customers with long histories about the rivers of Spain. But his tales, told in dialect, were less intelligible to me than those of the deaf-mute boy Alonso, who I also met in the market and whose restless face and body built up images like a silent movie. He described his family in mime, patting their several heads, and suddenly one could see them in a row beside him – his handsome father, his coughing consumptive mother, fighting brothers, and sly young sister. There was also a sickly baby, its head lolling back, and two dead ones, packed into little boxes – the boy set their limbs stiffly, sprinkled them with prayers, closed their eyes, and laid them away with a shrug.

In the market, too, I met Queipo, a beggar, whose hand had been bitten off by a mad dog in Madrid. Sometimes he'd lift up the red and wrinkled stump, bare his teeth, and bark at it savagely. Otherwise he was a rational companion, and showed me round the town and introduced me to the cheapest cafés. We used to meet at midday, count out our money, and spend it on wine and fishballs, then go down to the quayside, climb into a half-sunken boat, and doze through the afternoon.

The Seville quays were unpretentious, and seemed no more nautical than a coal-wharf in Birmingham. The Guadalquivir, at this point, was rather like the Thames at Richmond, and was about as busy as the Paddington Canal. Yet it was from this narrow river, fifty miles from the sea, that Columbus sailed to discover America, followed a few years later by the leaking caravelles of Magellan, one of which was the first to encircle the world. Indeed, the waterfront at Seville, with its paddling boys and orange-boats, and its mossy provincial stones, was for almost five hundred years – till the coming of space-aimed rockets – history's most significant launching-pad.

Queipo loved the quays. He wanted to go to Honolulu, he said. He pointed to his stump. 'But I can only swim in circles.' He had a family of fourteen, who lived in a cave in the country, and there was another child on the way. He spoke of his ageing wife with awe and impatience; she defeated all his attempts at control. 'I knew it was no good,' he growled, 'when she put that lace on her camisole.' She was over fifty, but still boundingly fertile. Two of his younger sons came into the city each day carrying a bucket wired to a pole, which Quiepo filled with meat-hash and orange skins and other scraps he'd begged from the cafés.

At night, when Queipo had returned to his cave, I'd walk back across the bridge to Triana, and sit on the cool flat roof of the Café Faro, and eat chips and gaze at the river. It seemed to be the only place in the city's bowl of heat where there was the slightest movement of air. The lights on the river collapsed, distended, and coiled hotly like electric eels. Sounds rose from the streets : the shouts of the sleepless children, the throb of music, an occasional scream. This was a city absorbed in a boxed life of its own; strangers were few and almost ignored. Seville lived for itself, split into two halves, one riding on the back of the other.

Until now, I'd accepted this country without question, as though visiting a half-crazed family. I'd seen the fat bug-eyed rich gazing glassily from their clubs, men scrabbling for scraps in the market, dainty upper-class virgins riding to church in carriages, beggar-women giving birth in doorways. Naïve and un-critical, I'd thought it part of the scene, not asking whether it was right or wrong. But it was in Seville, on the bridge, watch-ing the river at midnight, that I got the first hint of coming trouble. A young sailor approached me with a 'Hallo, Johnny', and asked for a cigarette. He spoke the kind of English he'd learnt on a Cardiff coal boat, spitting it out as though it hurt his tongue. 'I don't know who you are,' he said, 'but if you want to see blood, stick around – you're going to see plenty.'

# 9. East to Málaga

Life in Cádiz was too acrid to hold me for long, so after a few days I left it and turned eastwards at last, heading along the bare coastal shelf of Andalusia.

Behind me the white fish-hook bay impaled the last tides of the Atlantic, still smelling of herring shoals, but the milky green waves swept steadily towards the Straits through which

the Mediterranean would presently bloom. Already a generation old, I was still ignorant of the sea, unused to this sudden
unearthly neutrality, and the dizzy sweep of the water gave me
a feeling of vertigo, so that I kept carefully to the middle of the
road.

Between the mountains and the sea, the country was a dried-
up prairie, dun-coloured, smoking with dust. Thin wiry grass
bent to the day-long winds which covered them with a ghostly
film of salt, while far away to the north one could see the
black dots of bulls wandering over the plain like buffaloes.

I spent almost a week in this Arizona-type landscape. It
seemed forsaken, and most of the time I was alone. Sometimes
I met a solitary horseman, or a veiled woman on a donkey who
raised her hand to avert my evil eye. Or I would pass some
roadside villagers treading the dregs of their grapes in the sour
tail-end of the vintage. It was a joyless scene – the men and
girls, bare-legged, circling together in a kind of trance, stamping
the scummy vats with their blue-stained feet and uttering little
grunts and cries of exhaustion.

I remember sleeping one night in a hill-top cemetery, my
face stroked by the beams of a lighthouse, then taking breakfast next morning in a village wineshop where I heard the first
talk of war. The faces of the fishermen were dull and grey as
they rolled the harsh dry word between them. They spoke of
war in Abyssinia; meaningless to me, who hadn't seen a newspaper for almost three months.

Past Cape Trafalgar, the Straits narrowed visibly, the winds
died, and the sea grew calmer. Then Africa appeared, and the
skeins of the currents grew closer, crawling with little ships.
Between the jaws of two continents they met and mingled,
slowly filtering in and out, some heading back into the Mediterranean's calm blue womb, others breaking out into the grey
Atlantic.

I arrived at Tarifa, the southernmost point of Europe, to find
it still skulking behind its Arab walls. Once a Barbary stronghold and master of the Straits, it now lay stranded, a bit of
washed-up Africa, a decayed abstraction of Casbah-like alleys
wandering among blind and shuttered houses.

I found a café on the beach where I watched the sun go down, almost audibly, into a gulf of purple. The bar was crowded with fishermen, morose and silent, all gazing across the Straits. In the distant dusk one saw the orange smudge of Tangier break into little lights, then the night's heavy heat closed in upon us, prickling the face and hands.

The young fisherman at my table accepted a drink, and I asked him about the town. At first he was formal. 'It is very handsome,' he said; 'very historic, as you can see.' But he couldn't keep it up, and soon relaxed into truculence. 'It's like all the world. We have no work, no boats. The women prostrate themselves.'

We were joined quite soon by a mysterious dandy who invited us to share his bottle of whisky. He had rings on his fingers, wore a white silk shirt, and spoke English with an American accent. 'I am Cuban,' he said. 'You know the type. We are very wild kind of men. All we are innerested in is dames and revolutions – OK?' He wriggled with self-delight.

Suddenly he turned to the young fisherman, handed him a carton of cigarettes, and spoke to him in a rapid whisper. The fisherman listened, spat, shrugged his shoulders, then got up and went to the door. He whistled twice, and from the shadow of an upturned boat another shadow detached itself. The Cuban left the half-bottle of whisky behind him and went to the waiting girl on the beach.

The country east of Tarifa was high, bare, and brown as a mangy lion, with kites and vultures turning slowly overhead, square-winged, like electric fans. It was a scrub-covered wilderness, rippling with wind, but heartless, empty of life, except for occasional hunters who appeared suddenly with muskets, fired at nothing, then went away.

All day, as I climbed the twisting road, I heard the explosions rolling round the hills, the echoing crack of a gun followed by long empty silences like the fag-end of a war. At the top of the rise the country levelled into a kind of platform – a lofty gallery above the Straits – from which one could watch the slow blue currents of the Mediterranean snaking towards the

Atlantic's green forked tongue. Africa was now so near one could see the veins in the rocks running up the massive face of Morocco, with the afternoon sun peeling away the shadows to reveal deep and mysterious crevices. From Tangier, the panorama swept east to Ceuta and back into the mint-green hills of the Rif – the Barbary Coast, inscrutable threshold of violence, which made me feel capable of extreme adventures.

Instead I slept for an hour in the withered gorse, and woke to find a gunman standing over me. 'How d'you do?' I said foolishly, flustered, in English. The man giggled, and crept away.

Later the mountain road dropped into a narrow valley full of sea-mist and stunted cork trees, where flocks of damp sheep with long Cotswold faces wandered among strands of glittering cobwebs. The place was green and chill, curiously familiar, like a pocket of western England. And sure enough, as I climbed to the next high peak, there was Gibraltar crouching low in the distance.

Africa, Spain, and the great sweep of the bay, all shone with a fierce bronze light. But not Gibraltar; it lay apart like an interloper, as though it had been towed out from Portsmouth and anchored off-shore still wearing its own grey roof of weather. Slate-coloured, aloof, surrounded by a scattering of warships and fringed by its dock-yard cranes, the Rock lay shadowed beneath a plate of cloud, immersed in a private rain-storm.

I went no farther that night, but camped out on the hill-top, content to stay where I was. The vista below me spread from Ronda to the Rif, a classical arrangement of sea and rock, with the mouth of the Mediterranean pierced by the wash of ships tracing a course as old as Homer. Kites and kestrels swung silently overhead, smouldering in the evening sun; and as twilight approached, the Pillars of Hercules turned purple and the sea poured between them in a flush of lavender. Alone, with my back to a sun-warmed rock, I finished the last of my food, gazing where Africa and Europe touched finger-tips in this merging of day and night.

Suddenly it was dark, and Gibraltar became a heap of

diamonds, and Algeciras stretched out claws of light. Then a huge moon rose straight out of the sea, and hung motionless, like a frozen bloom. The wind rose too, funnelling from the Atlantic, and I wrapped in my blanket, shivering with cold.

The Port of Algeciras had a potency and charm which I'd found nowhere else till then. It was a scruffy little town built round an open drain and smelling of fruit skins and rotten fish. There were a few brawling bars and modest brothels; otherwise the chief activity was smuggling. At most street-corners one would be offered exotic items of merchandise unavailable anywhere else in Spain – mouldy chocolate, laddered stockings, damp American cigarettes, leaky Parkers, and fake Swiss watches.

But for all its disreputable purposes and confidence-trickery, it seemed to be a town entirely free of malice, and even the worst of its crooks were so untrained in malevolence that no one was expected to take them seriously. In its position as a bridge between Europe and Morocco, the port could have equalled Marseilles in evil, but its heart wasn't in it, in spite of the opportunities, and it preferred small transgressions with lesser rewards.

Algeciras was a clearing-house for odds and ends, and I stayed there about two weeks. I remember the fishing boats at dawn bringing in tunny from the Azores, the markets full of melons and butterflies, the international freaks drinking themselves into multi-lingual stupors, the sly yachts running gold to Tangier ... I spent part of my time with a gang of youths who earned their living spiking handbags with fish-hooks, who got rid of their loot in the bars and brothels, and begged their meals at the local convent. The leader of the gang was a 'globe-trotter' from Lisbon, who claimed to be walking round the world. But he was always slipping back home to fetch something he'd forgotten and had taken two years to get as far as this.

For myself, I thought it best to stick to the fiddle, and here the town was rewarding enough. My patrons were varied, and their approach was direct. I was often taken aside and asked for a favourite tune. Schubert, for some reason, was most popular here, followed by local ballads of mystical sex. One night I was taken to a boat to play to a Chinese cook, who baked me a bag of biscuits in return. I was also asked for 'On With the Motley' by a Cardiff stoker, and 'Ave Maria' by a party of drunken priests. Another night a young smuggler invited me to serenade his invalid mistress, after which I was rewarded with a wrist-watch which ticked madly for an hour and then exploded in a shower of wheels.

I was half in love with Algeciras and its miniature villainies, and felt I could have stayed on there indefinitely. But part of my plan at that time was still to follow the coast round Spain, so I had to leave it and get on to Málaga.

But first of all there remained the question of Gibraltar, only twenty minutes across the bay. Too near to resist, I thought I'd drop in for the afternoon, present my passport, and have some tea. The old paddle-wheel ferry carried me across the water, smooth as oil and leaping with dolphins, while I enjoyed the boat's brief passage of tax-free drinking, with brandy a penny a glass.

To travellers from England, Gibraltar is an Oriental bazaar, but coming in from Spain I found it more like Torquay – the same helmeted police, tall angular women, and a cosy smell of provincial groceries. I'd forgotten how much the atmosphere of home depended on white bread, soap, and soup-squares. Even in this conclave of Maltese–Genoese–Indians, one sensed the pressure of cooking-steam.

My welcome at the colony was not what I expected. The port officials looked me up and down with doubt. The rest of the travellers were passed briskly through the barrier while I was put on one side like an infected apple. Clipped phone-calls were made to remoter authorities, warily seeking advice. 'Oh, his passport's all right. No, he's not broke, exactly. Well, you know ... Well, sort of ... Yes ...'

Finally I was taken in a truck to see the Chief of Police, a worried but kindly man. 'But who *are* you?' he kept saying. 'It's rather difficult here. You must try to realize our position. It doesn't *do*, you know – if you'll forgive my saying so. Nothing personal, you understand ...'

Anyway, it was agreed that I could stay for a day or two, if I slept in the police station, where they could keep an eye on me. So I was given a clean little cell, a cake of soap, and I played dominoes with the prisoners in the evenings. I wasn't under arrest, exactly; I was allowed out in the daytime so long as I reported back at night. But the restriction was tedious, and after a few days of bacon and eggs, a policeman conducted me back to the frontier.

Leaving Gibraltar was like escaping from an elder brother in charge of an open jail. I crossed the land-bridge at La Linea and climbed up to San Roque – exiled home of the Spanish mayors of Gibraltar. Looking back, I could see the Rock still capped by its cloud, grey as a gun-turret, dripping with mist – while the mainland around lay under the beating sun, jagged with mountains as blue as clinkers. Spain enclosed me once more with its anarchic indifference, asking no discipline but the discipline of manners. I was back on the road, cushioned by its unswept dust, and by my anonymity, which would raise no eyebrows.

It took five days to Málaga, walking the switch-back road between the mountains and the sea, five days pushing on through the dazzling light to a reek of hot seaweed, thyme, and shellfish. I passed through occasional cork-woods smoking with the camp-fires of gypsies squatting by little streams, through scented beanfields rushing with milky water and villages screened under veils of fishnets. Ruined watch-towers, some fluttering with sleepy ravens, marked the headlands along the way, while below them the rocks and the sea lay motionless, locked together in a fume of heat.

Nothing moved inland except the running channels of water laid out by the Moors eight centuries before. The road rippled before me, and distant villages in the mountains shone like pinches of salt on silk. Sometimes, leaving the road, I would walk into the sea and pull it voluptuously over my head, and stand momentarily drowned in the cool blind silence, in a salt-stung neutral nowhere.

When twilight came I slept where I was, on the shore or some rock-strewn headland, and woke to the copper glow of the rising sun coming slowly across the sea. Mornings were pure resurrection, which I could watch sitting up, still wrapped like a corpse in my blanket, seeing the blood-warm light soak back into the sierras, slowly re-animating their ash-grey cheeks, and feeling the cold of the ground drain away beneath me as the sunrise reached my body.

Then from far out to sea, through the melting mist, would emerge a white-sailed fishing fleet, voiceless, timeless, quiet as air, drifting inshore like bits of paper. But they were often ships of despair; they brought little with them, perhaps a few baskets of poor sardines. The women waited, then turned and went away in silence. The red-eyed fishermen threw themselves down on the sand.

The road to Málaga followed a beautiful but exhausted shore, seemingly forgotten by the world. I remember the names – San Pedro, Estepona, Marbella, and Fuengirola. ... They were salt-fish villages, thin-ribbed, sea-hating, cursing their place in the sun. At that time one could have bought the whole coast for a shilling. Not Emperors could buy it now.

From its name, I expected Málaga to be a kind of turreted stronghold, half Saracen, half Corsair-pirate. Instead I found an untidy city on the banks of a dried-up river, facing a modern commercial harbour, the streets full of cafés and slummy bars, and its finest building the Post Office.

I stayed at an inn by the dried-up river, where I shared a courtyard with about a dozen families. Cooking went on all day at their separate fires, in pots mounted on little stones. The reek of fat and charcoal was always in the nostrils, giving one a pungent sense of well-being – though the presence of the fires was more comforting than the food, which was usually a gruel of unmentionable scraps.

But the posada was home, and I bedded down in my place with the mules and wives and children. Honour, not modesty, was what we lived by here, together with a watchful sense of protection. Food and drink might be shared at any time, but each man's goods were sacred – these could be left all day, piled in a heap by the wall, and no one, not even a dog, would touch them.

The courtyard was mostly occupied by mountain people who had come down to the city to sell baskets and cloth – the beautiful hand-woven blankets of the Alpujarras, half Arab, half Mexican in style, decorated with bold abstractions in scarlet and black or sprinkled with geometrical peacocks.

The men of the Alpujarras were wiry as Bulgars, but with hazed out-of-focus eyes, as though being cooped up in the city and temporarily robbed of their distances had also robbed them of their power of sight. The women dressed in stiff garments of black and tan, which gave them the look of Homeric Greeks, while the young girls were the most graceful I'd ever seen, light-footed and nimble as deer, with long floating arms and articulate bodies which turned every movement into a ritual dance. When at rest they would stand, narrow hips thrust sideways, instinctively forming a saddle for child or water-jar, half-shading their eyes with a leaf-brown hand as though still dazzled by the Sierra snows.

Squatting together in the courtyard, on the dung-coated cobbles, we were like a wandering tribe at rest. There would be shouts, cries, snarls, and laughter, mixed with the formal obscenities and blessings. 'Carmencita! Come! – I pollute your mother...' 'A pinch of salt? – what grace and sympathy.' 'May my testicles wither, but I agree with you, man...' 'God's codpiece, you're very kind...'

Old women, as shrivelled as carob beans, joined in the shouting with tongues like razors; or sat watchfully chewing with that timeless rhythm of the aged, folding their faces like old felt hats. The children ran free, squirming under the horses, half-naked in their grimy vests. The men sat apart, smoking and drinking, mending a sandal or piece of harness, talking ceaselessly together with the dry throaty rattle of pebbles being rolled down a gulley.

When it rained I would spend the whole day in their company, sitting under the gallery, watching the heavy sky. The mules steamed gently, the balconies dripped. We drew closer, bored but secure. A woman mended my shirt and folded it up at my feet. Another asked questions about my sisters. A child of eight knelt beside me and peered into the holes of my ears. 'Maria, cuño, do not molest the Frenchman!' Sometimes a half-mad girl stood weeping in the rain while the men teased and taunted her. The huge eyes puckered, melting with slow slack tears. She made no attempt to escape.

When night came, the light bulbs were dim and ghostly. People sank back into their shadows. Eyes only were visible, touched by the red of the fires, sleepily slatted like the eyes of bats. Blankets were spread on the stones, families stretched out together – the girls in the centre with the younger children. Everyone sighed and settled, curling up on their sides, talk dying with the dying fires. Then nothing would be heard but the occasional shudder of a mule, the sudden wrestling of man and wife.

The rains stopped, and I went out again with the fiddle and began playing under the dripping palm trees. Málaga was full of foreigners – effeminate Dutch, sandy Germans, mackin-toshed Frenchmen, and English debs. I lazily wandered among them playing tunes of all nations and being rewarded with drinks and money. Most of the visitors, it was clear, were not strangers to each other, but formed a snug expatriate colony, moving from table to table, bar to bar, in constantly changing liaisons.

All, that is, save the English debs, who sat separately, wear-ing little hats, keeping one eye on the Consul and talking musi-cally of Mummy while sipping glasses of pallid tea. Seeing them under the palms in the warm autumn haze, cool as doves in their tennis white, what hungers they started for their cream-of-wheat textures, tang of toothpaste around the lips, and that particular rainswept grey of their English eyes, only noticeable when abroad.

But it was the young Germans, a complex and mysterious crowd, who outnumbered the rest of the colony. Most seemed to be engaged in inexplicable errands and few were as poor as they looked. But they were friendly enough, and I began to see quite a lot of them in their hideouts behind the cathedral.

There was Karl, from Hamburg, for whom I wrote love-letters. (He loved Mrs Lucas, an English widow.) And Heinz, a teacher (said to be a stool-pigeon and agent, though I never gathered for what). There were also three Bavarians who paraded the streets in sackcloth and sandals as though on their way to the scaffold. And Walter and Shulamith, two Jewish refugees, who had walked from Berlin carrying their one-year-old child. I see them today as part of the shadow of the times, and most of them obviously led double lives. They suspected me too, and were always trying to catch me out, hinting at roles I was supposed to be playing. But for all their apparent gaiety and solidarity as a group, they were more suspicious of one another.

The moist hot days began to fill up the city with a kind of amiable lethargy. Gypsies from the river started to rob the markets, and nobody tried to stop them. Children swarmed in the belfries, madly ringing the bells, and nobody interfered. Even the mules stopped working and wandered aimlessly round the streets like sightseers in from the country.

One stifling midday I decided to climb to the Castle to get some air and perhaps a view of the sea. Hovels scattered the hillside, stacked one above the other, and women sat on the doorsteps fanning themselves with cardboard. They flashed bright gold teeth when they saw me coming, and called out friendly invitations. Then one of them beckoned me indoors and offered me her giant daughter, who lay sprawled on a huge brass bed. The sight of the girl and the bed, packed into that tiny room, was like some familiar 'Alice' nightmare. I could only smile and stutter, clutching the doorpost and pretending not to understand. 'Love!' cried the mother, shaking the bed till it rattled, while the girl bounced slowly like a basking whale. I complimented the woman and made some excuse, saying that it was too early in the day. 'Light of heaven!' she cried, 'what else is there to do?' Fortunately, it was impossible even to get into the room.

Much of destitute Málaga, like this hillside slum, lived directly off the dockyard. By day the poor went to the ships for food; at night the sailors came into the town. I met a group of them one evening, straight off a British tanker, four short little battered men, who I saw straggling down a street in single file calling to each other like ships in a fog. 'Where we goin' then, Geordie?' 'Dunno, Jock – bash on.' They were carrying bars of carbolic soap.

I took them to a tavern at the back of the market, where we swapped the soap for bottles of brandy. The local soap, at that time, was like millstone grit, and ships' carbolic was better than money. With the drink in their hands, the sailors relaxed, opened their shirts, and began to beam and sweat. Their talk built up quickly in spurts of dialect; vigorous, clipped, and funny; composed of that fusillade of fantasy, filth, and insult which marked them together as British mates.

Jock, Geordie, Lenny, and Bill; two were from Liverpool, two from Glasgow. They were all older than I was, yet they addressed me with careful courtesy, tempering their oaths as they did so. But their main concern, having come safely ashore, was that they should get enough to drink. So they drank like maniacs, their faces shining with purpose, grabbing bottles, knocking over glasses, mixing brandy, anis, wine, and beer in one frantic obliterating rout.

Semi-paralysis was the target, and there were no middle stages, no songs or tears or fights. Geordie, the stoker, was the first to go, sliding slowly down from his chair. 'Y'know, I loved that woman,' he said from the floor. 'I loved that woman, y'know. Know what I mean? . . .' He clutched the leg of a passing fisherman. 'It's the truth – I loved that woman . . .' Jock and Bill soon joined him, blank-eyed and speechless, falling crumpled across each other. Then it was Lenny's turn. 'I'm on duty,' he said, got up, and walked into the wall.

It was long after midnight when I got them back to their ship and stowed them away in their bunks. I was far gone too, and the watchman let me sleep on board – that is, if he noticed the difference. The next morning the sailors were bright as larks, plunging their heads into buckets of water. 'Up the spout we was, the lot of us.' They gave me a breakfast of mutton chops.

\*

The rains returned, with great black thunderstorms rolling daily in from the sea. So I exchanged the exposure of the open courtyard at the inn for a six-bedded room upstairs, where for a peseta a night one could sleep in damp grey sheets under a bent and dripping roof. My companions were artists from a travelling circus, temporarily stranded by the weather, including an asthmatic ventriloquist who talked in his sleep (and ours), four dwarfs who shared one bed, and a white-whiskered bird-tamer who slept by himself, fully clothed, in top hat and boots.

Another inmate was Avelino, a student from Ronda, who occupied a dark little room down the passage. He was a tense young man, with the soft eyes of a lemur and a tormented blue-furred face. He used to creep nervously about on the tips of his toes, fingering a rosary made of plumstones.

Perhaps he saw in me someone lost to heaven, a sorry exile without god or country; anyway, I soon became the object of his inexhaustible attention, a chosen burden for charity.

Tirelessly, speechless, and self-effacing, for a week he was my day-long shadow. If I was eating in a café, I'd see him watching me from the doorway, and when I left I'd find that he'd paid the bill. If I was fiddling in the street, he'd march silently up and down, dropping pennies into my hat as he passed. If I was writing in my room he'd suddenly steal up behind me and place a lighted cigarette between my lips.

There were also the discreet little gifts I'd find laid on my bed: a bunch of flowers, some tobacco, a shirt; and then one morning, a poem, neatly pinned to the pillow, freshly written in a copper-plate hand: 'He sleeps, the young man, far from his home and people, forgetting his doleful life, not knowing that tomorrow his music will be torn by the winds and scattered above the rooftops.'

At the end of the week, Avelino broke his silence, saying that he'd worked out a plan for our future. He would start a school, and I would join him. He'd teach Ethics and Philosophy; and I, English and Art – and so take my proper place in the world. 'You would wear a suit and cravat, and walk proudly in the streets, and bow to your friends and call

"Adios". And they would reply "Adios", and give you respects. It would be cultured and very gracious . . .'

His voice suddenly faded. He tore a crucifix from his shirt, covered it with kisses, and fled from the room. They told me next morning that he'd gone back to Ronda, having given his money and clothes to the porter.

During my last days in Málaga I was faced by a near disaster – my violin suddenly broke in my hands. Over-exposure to the sun seemed to have weakened the joints, and the instrument simply fell to pieces.

Friends at the posada did what they could to help, melting glue in their cooking pots. The violin, which by now looked like a mess of chicken-bones, was reassembled and the joints reset. For several days it lay strapped-up under my bed, rolled in sacking and weighted with stones. But the joints wouldn't hold, and as soon as the strings were tightened, the whole thing fell apart again.

I was anxious. Without the violin I knew of no other way to live, and I would soon be out of money. It had all been too easy, wherever I happened to be, scraping out a few odd tunes for a meal; now I wandered round Málaga in a kind of daze, as though I'd lost the use of my hands. There seemed only one thing to be done – join the crew of some ship, leave Spain, and perhaps go back home.

Fortunately, this wasn't necessary. A liner arrived in the bay carrying five hundred British tourists, and I set up as a guide, arranging for cut-rate taxis, English teas, and excursions to the hills. I was doing quite well, and thought this might see me through the winter, when the local guides ganged up on me. If I didn't go back to my fiddle-playing, they said, they would throw me into the harbour.

So I was stuck again. But another stroke of luck saved me. I met a young German from the School of Languages. Did I know anyone, by chance, who wanted a violin? He had one he didn't need. It belonged to his girl friend and she'd run off with a Swede. He gave it to me for nothing.

# 10. Castillo

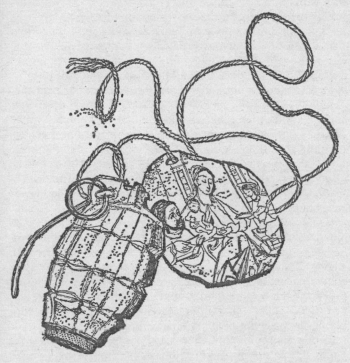

As December closed in I decided to hole-up for the winter at Castillo, sixty miles east of Málaga. It was a tumbling little village built on an outcrop of rock in the midst of a pebbly delta, backed by a bandsaw of mountains and fronted by a grey strip of sand which some hoped would be an attraction for tourists.

There were two hotels, one of them run by a Swiss, who offered me hospitality in return for certain odd-job duties, which included helping in the kitchen, mending doors and windows, and playing the violin in the saloon at night. The hotel was new, but had been built on the beach, so that the waves broke over the windows, and already the fine concrete walls were beginning to crumble and the proprietor was drawn with worry.

Herr Brandt must have been something of a pioneer on the coast, but he'd arrived twenty years too soon, and I found him on the verge of a nervous breakdown, convinced that his investment was at the mercy of anarchists. He was always washing his hands, then washing the soap, and changing all the locks on the doors. But he was resourceful, almost desperate, at running his business, and while the neighbouring hotel shut down for the winter he was determined to keep his going, turning its booming rooms into a centre for the local gentry, for musical teas, buffet suppers, and dancing.

So I was enrolled on the staff and encouraged to get some new clothes. Then I was given a room in the attic with a Jewish boy from Cologne – 'Don Jacobo', as the housemaids called him.

Jacobo was in his twenties, short and tubby, with a Hitler moustache and a rubbery bounce. Already bald at the crown, he had a tuft of hair on his forehead which rose and fell with emotion, and had to be plastered in place with heavy slicks of oil and sometimes even with lard. He was a boon to Herr Brandt, acting as interpreter, tout, hotel secretary, boot-boy, and gigolo. He also played the accordion which, together with my fiddle, made up the hotel band.

Jacobo spoke English with slapdash gusto, worrying the words like a terrier. The first time I met him he was on his hands and knees, pawing frantically through a pile of laundry. 'This morning,' he said, 'I am having many disgusts with the washwife – she has forlorn me my new chemise. And tonight, you see, I was having a girl from the village – she was coming from suppertime.'

He knew everyone in Castillo and everyone liked him. He could be convincing in several languages. He had a kind of liquorice charm, both yielding and elastic, and in spite of his looks was considered a dandy.

I remember being woken late one night, soon after I arrived, to find him powdering his head in the mirror. He was dressed in a long blue gown, like a Chinaman, and smelt richly of exotic oils. Seeing he'd disturbed me, he gave a fat little giggle and laid a finger along his lips.

'Say nothing, my friend. I am expecting downstairs. Anybody is waiting for me in this hotel.'

Anybody, it seemed, was a widow from Paris, who'd come for the day and stayed three weeks, during which we spent a succession of broken nights, with Jacobo on call like a doctor.

Each morning we practised together on the roof, working up a selection of musical tit-bits. Jacobo was a nimble accordionist and played the instrument with windy pleasure; it seemed well suited to his pneumatic passions. Quite soon we'd developed a reasonable repertoire, enough to satisfy Herr Brandt's demands – operatic arias for the tea-rooms, serenades for the evening, pasodobles and tangos for dancing.

The Sunday before Christmas we gave our first Grand Concert, but this was ruined by exploding wine-bottles, a series of reverberating incidents due to faulty supplies which put our audience in disarray. We had somewhat more success with our weekend dances, which were held in a kind of white-tiled washhouse downstairs. These were formal affairs, full of suppressed sexuality, but controlled by rigid Andalusian manners. The chaperoned girls sat on display round the walls, pretty as coloured paper, quivering to the music with butterfly vibrations which soon brought the young men in from the night. Approaches could only be made through a watchful third party – mother, brother, or aunt – but the dances, though stilted, concealed much emotional grappling, and for a while were the height of fashion.

Castillo itself, built of stone steps from the delta, was grey, almost gloomily Welsh. The streets were steep, roughly paved, and crossed by crude little arches, while the square was like a cobbled farmyard. Part of the castle was a cemetery, part of the Town Hall a jail, but past glories were eroding fast.

In the days of the Moors, Castillo had been a front-line fortress standing high in the mouth of the delta, guarding the rich river valley which wound up through the Sierra towards the islamic paradise of Granada. Several centuries later, it was also the point of farewell for the defeated Caliphs when they were driven from Spain, and a wave-battered cross standing on an off-shore rock celebrated the spot where they sailed away.

Apart from a few merchants, landowners, and officials from Granada, everybody now in the village was poor, and the ruined castle on the hill seemed to serve as a perpetual reminder that not they, but someone else, had conquered. The peasants had only two ways of living, and both were loaded against them – the sugar canes and the offshore fishing.

The strip of dirty grey sand dividing the land from the sea was a frontier between two kinds of poverty. The sugar canes in the delta, rustling dryly in the wind, were a deception even at harvest time, for the best they could offer was a few weeks' work and in the meantime the men stood idle.

But the land was rich compared with the sea, which nourished only a scattering of poor sardines. There were no boats or equipment for deep-sea fishing, the village was chained to the offshore wastes, shallow, denuded, too desperately fished to provide anything but constant reproaches.

I remember the cold red mornings, just before sunrise, when the fishermen came down to the beach, padding softly through the mist in their rope-soled shoes, or bare-footed, with feet like ink. Two boats would put out into the sullen sea, indigo shadows against the dawn, while the men rowed madly, dipping their long oars deep and calling hoarsely to one another.

At least thirty more men would remain waiting ashore, watching the rowers with screwed-up eyes. The boats were racing the fish, paying the net out fast in an attempt to encircle what few there were. Painfully they spread it across the sea in a long and bobbing line, then turned and rowed back, dragging the two loose ends – which was when the men on the beach went to work.

In two teams, trousers rolled, they splashed into the waves and seized each end of the sagging net. Then for an hour they hauled in, panting their way up the beach, bent double, clawing the sand with their toes, the leaders running back to join the end of the line, each man silent, his face to the ground. The two long files of fishermen trudging out of the water might have been coolies or Egyptian slaves, slowly drawing behind them the weight of a net which encircled almost a quarter of a mile of sea.

It was labour without mercy, dignity, or reward, and the men hauled at the net without hope, each one grunting and straining in the horizontal position of a beast, his face to the buttocks of the man in front. It was a grinding hour of expended strength, too mindless even for comradeship. When the cod-end at last had been dragged ashore, the men gathered round it in silence, while the few kilos of sardines, a heap of dirty silver, died flickering in the sand.

The auctioneer arrived, unshaven, in his pyjamas, and a dismal price was set. Perhaps fifty pesetas – half to the owner of the boats and the rest between forty men. Sometimes the price was so low that no sale was made, and the men divided the fish between them, slowly counting them out into forty little heaps, a sandy fistful for each man's family.

Set against this background, the hotel on the beach was a tawdry interjection, out of scale and taste. I continued to work and sleep there, and eat my meals, but spent as much time as I could in the village.

It had little to offer, except for the people, who had all the time in the world. The little cavelike shops had almost nothing to sell save sandals and sunflower seeds; strangely enough there was a bookshop, though it only had four books – Milton, Homer, Andreyev, and Machado.

Physically, the villagers showed the strong Arab blood which the Catholic conquest had been unable to dispel – the old women stark and black as desert matriarchs, their bodies loaded with unhealthy fat; the men small and bony, like dried-up birds, perched moodily round the edge of the sea. The men spent much of the day just staring at their hands and sucking cigarettes made of beech leaves – a tongue-blistering smoke flavoured with the juice of sugar cane and some hot harsh root from the hills. The only people with jobs seemed to be the village girls, most of them in service to the richer families, where for a bed in a cupboard and a couple of pounds a year they were expected to run the whole house and keep the men from the brothels.

As elsewhere on the coast, the villagers were infected with fatalism, a kind of subdued and deliberate apathy. Only sometimes in the eyes of the younger men did one see the violent hopes they lived for. The children, on the other hand, were a different race, inhabiting a brief but confident gaiety – beautiful verminous creatures with strong white teeth and diseased red-lidded eyes. Prancing about in their rags, snatching what food they could get, they never whined but lived on charm, were pampered, indulged, and smothered with easy love, and punished only for rude manners to strangers.

The bad weather came, the hills disappeared in mist, and the village began to look more like Wales than ever. Gutters splashed and gurgled, people crept about in sacking, and the rain fell solidly, like cold wet lead.

There were no clients in the hotel, no boats on the sea, so I went like everybody else to the bars. Here I'd find Manolo the waiter, Felipe the chef, and 'Gambas' the crippled porter, and always a group of young fishermen with wet sand on their feet, and a few labourers down from the farms. We drank crude brandy mixed with boiling water, often a cheaper drink than wine, and ate morunos – little dishes of hot pig flesh, cut from the fat and stewed in sauce.

Mostly we talked, with the rain drumming the windows and the drinks steaming along the bar. Conversations were oblique, full of hints and proverbs, well guarded by careful custom. Figures in authority were never exactly named but referred to in cipher, usually by their sexual parts. Opinions and judgements were also cloaked in metaphor, phrases of folklore dipped from a common well.

'He who sleeps with a dog gets up with fleas.'

'Horns are visible to every man but the wearer.'

Or when the barmaid, carrying washing, stumbled on to an old man's lap: 'God always sends nuts to the toothless.'

During those cold soggy days, ducking from bar to bar, one

met the usual town eccentrics. There was Manolo's brother, who always carried a pebble in his mouth because it prolonged the taste of the brandy. And Jorge, who'd trained a sparrow to sip other men's drinks and then carry them to his mouth by the beakful. When the bird died, said Jorge, he would weep weep, weep. Every man in the bar agreed. There was also Pau, a young fisherman who was teaching himself to write by using the tavern wall as a copybook, but who sometimes exploded with frustration and beat the wall with his fist till his knuckles ran with blood.

Occasionally a day turned unhealthy, when idleness and ennui led to an outburst of mirthless riot. Then the village idiot would be seized, and strapped to a chair, and tormented until he screamed. Wine would be poured on his head, or a man would hold him by the ears while another spread his face with mustard. After a session of this everyone looked flushed and relaxed. Even the Civil Guard would come in to watch.

At other times the men would grow quiet and gentle, standing with arms round each other's shoulders, someone singing in a voice that seemed to come from far away, a muted falsetto cry. In spite of our long hours in the bars there was almost no drunkenness, perhaps due to the spacious rhythm of our drinking. But being less used to the brandy, it would sometimes hit me hard, till I found myself staring at the room in wonder. I'd see a gypsy come in wearing a great red mouth as though he'd bitten into a harvest moon. Such were moments of that pure, almost virginal intoxication, to which all subsequent drinking tries in vain to return.

Manolo the waiter protected me when I was drunk and humoured me like a grandfather. One night, I remember, during a particularly flashy thunderstorm, the sky spitting with electric sparks, he telephoned the lighthouse and asked them to stop fooling about, saying the Englishman didn't like it ...

Manolo was about thirty years old, handsome as a playboy, but moody and idealistic. He was the leader of a group of fishermen and labourers into which I was gradually admitted. We met in a pink-washed room at the back of the bar and talked about the world to come – a world without church or government or army, where each man alone would be his private government.

It was a simple, one-syllable view of life, as black and white as childhood, and as Manolo talked, the fishermen listened, bobbing their heads up and down like corks. Their fathers had never heard or known such promises. Centuries of darkness stood behind them. Now it was January 1936, and these things were suddenly thinkable, possible, even within their reach.

But first, said Manolo, there must be death and dissolution; much had to be destroyed and cleared away. Felipe, the chef, who liked food and girls, was the pacifier, preaching love and reason. No guns, he said; they dishonoured the flesh; and no destruction, which dishonoured the mind. Everyone knew, all the same, that there were now guns in the village which hadn't been there before.

Life must start clean, Manolo said, if only for the children's sake. Not till the tyrants had been destroyed, and their infection burnt from the ground, could love and freedom etcetera ... His apocalyptic phrases fell like hammer strokes – but every so often the spirit went out of him. Then he would double up at the table as if in sudden pain, beating his fists together. 'They'll stop us,' he'd groan. 'They'll bring in the army. We haven't got a chance.'

Behind the radiant plans and surges of optimism, hovered this sick and desperate disquiet. All of them seemed to feel it at some time or other, and it made their meetings even more tragic. In spite of the naïve abstractions, these were councils of war, aimed at the local enemy they knew. Sometimes Manolo would come in with his pockets bulging with pamphlets, which he'd spread carefully around the table. They were crudely printed, on ash-grey paper, but might have been tablets handed down from the Prophets. Each man would pore over them, stroking the letters or slowly spelling out the words. The fraternal greetings in scarlet, the drawings of heroic workers with banners, were strange new myths in their lives. So was the spirited advice on the reorganizing of farms and fisheries once victory was won. Yet they knew, as they read, that this was no easy paradise. The village would burn for it first.

'Lorenzo,' said Manolo, with a touch of shame in his voice. 'We are going to need the help of all the world.'

Winter went out with the 'kissing of Christ's feet', preceded by a sombre procession with torches. The black-edged notices had gone up around the village, jostling the grafitti for revolution – 'Besapies al Santissimo Cristo de la Buena Muerte en su Capilla de la Patrona.' Sacred Christ of the Good Death, in the Chapel on the hill, in a cleft of rock just below the castle.

The women and girls came wailing through the streets, stumbling barefooted over the slaty cobbles, bearing the terrible image upon their shoulders like a drowned man brought from the sea. The Christ was carved from old wood the colour of moonlight, transfixed in a rigor of ugly death, his wounds wetly shining with fresh red paint, his face cavernous and decomposed.

The women took it in turns, bent double like crones and gasping under their load, jerking the awkward figure round the narrow corners while its nailed arms scraped along the walls. Most of the men, it seemed, had stayed away that night; this was an occasion for female mourning. The pitch-pine torches dripped and bubbled, and fires of brushwood dotted the hill. A high-pitched wailing possessed the village, threading moodily among the houses, while the flames of the torches threw up primitive shadows, giant flickerings of garish light, covering the women's faces with convulsive masks, half sorrow, half grinning gargoyle.

I followed the procession till it reached the chapel, where a stern young priest was waiting. The Crucifix was propped among stones and surrounded by flares. The women went down on their knees. Then the priest addressed us, saying how unique were the faithful and how damned the materialists of today. There were cries of 'Piedad!', 'Señor!', and 'Salvame!', and lilies were tied to the feet of the Christ. He towered woodenly above us in the light of the torches, his toes already shining from the lips of the women.

*

In February came the Election, with a victory for the socialists. This was not deliverance, merely a letting up of confusion. An end to years of listening and waiting for something to happen. Suddenly everything was out in the open.

A Popular Front, they said; a People's Government at last. Manolo went about with his face lit up. The peasants and fishermen stood all day in the plaza, talking more openly now, but tense. The result of the election had given them power, but it was still too hot to grasp. The news, in fact, was not victory for anyone but a declaration of war.

Castillo, like Spain, was split down the middle, and the two sides drew apart, on guard. Little happened at first – the fishermen took over a boat, the peasants commandeered some land. Meanwhile the owners lay low and sat whispering in the casino, peering through the curtained windows, and waiting.

Spring came in with a rush of snow-water from the Sierras which carried a long red stain out to sea. A young girl died and was taken round in an open coffin on a last visit from house to house. I remember her smooth quiet face, as green as moss, and the cotton wool in her nostrils like puffs of frozen breath.

A kind of brilliant green film suddenly broke over the fields, sheets of wild flowers covering the dried-up hills – orchids spiking the dust, rocks crowned with anemones, almond blossom exploding like popcorn. The uneasiness in the village was part of this spring, like a rush of blood to the head, bringing with it a curious relaxation of behaviour and manners, a new freedom among the sexes.

Jacobo and I still organized the hotel dances, but their flavour was different now. Gone were the stiff and sweltering little marriage markets, with their chaperones and wax-haired suitors; now the floor was commanded by young fishermen and labourers, casual in sky-blue shirts, who swung their cotton-dressed girls through the stamping fox-trots in an embrace of assured possession.

Herr Brandt, more jumpy and nervous than ever, read the signs and admitted them free. They drank the cheap fizzy beer rather than the high-toned sherry, and Manolo served them with comradely pride. Together with the chef and the porter

he more or less ran the hotel now, and treated Herr Brandt
with scrupulous insolence, too proud to rob him, but making it
clear all the same that these new clients were the only ones
that mattered.

So the boys and girls of Castillo used our rackety dances to
explore their new-found liberties. During the warm spring
evenings they clung earnestly together, as though intimacy was
a new invention, dancing, holding hands, or walking in couples
along the shore, arms entwined, watching each other's faces.

There were also other freedoms. Books and films appeared,
unmutilated by Church or State, bringing to the peasants of the
coast, for the first time in generations, a keen breath of the
outside world. For a while there was a complete lifting of
censorship, even in newspapers and magazines. But most of all
it was the air of carnality, the brief clearing away of taboos,
which seemed to possess the village – a sudden frank, even
frantic, pursuit of lust, bred from a sense of impending peril.

Early one morning I got word from Manolo asking me to
meet him in a bar. I found him head down in a corner with two
comrades from Málaga, diminutive and clerk like men.

'Lorenzo,' said Manolo. 'We want you to do something for
us.'

The strangers looked at me doubtfully.

'If he can do it, that is.'

'Of course he can do it,' said Manolo. 'He has legs like a bull.
Mountains are nothing to him.'

It was simple enough; they wanted me to take an innocent-
sounding message to a farmer up in the hills, telling him when
to expect a delivery of seed-potatoes – in other words, hand-
grenades.

'You're always walking about,' Manolo said dryly. 'Of course
you'll be seen, but no one will wonder.'

I said I'd go, so they drew me a Red Indian map, dotted with
rocks and streams and haystacks, with a series of arrows leading through fishbone forests to the lonely farm on the hill. It
was about eight miles inland, at the foot of the Sierra; somewhere I'd always wanted to go. Manolo gave me a half-bottle of

coñac, and I set out through the fresh spring landscape, which was full of the sound of gushing water.

The journey took about three hours and I saw no one on the way, only congregations of dishevelled storks, who kept dropping out of the sky like wind-blown umbrellas and stumbling about in disorder. The map was all right as far as it went, but suddenly the path petered out in a bog. I could see the farm just ahead, but found there was a flooded river between us which Manolo hadn't bothered to mention.

At that moment a young man crept out of breast-high reeds as though he'd been expecting me. He gave me a quick sharp look, then shouted across the river:

'From Castillo! Send Ignacio!'

I saw the farm door open and a woman run out. Then a horseman appeared and galloped down the hill. Without drawing rein, he reached the bank of the river, plunged in, and swam across towards me.

Horse and rider for a moment seemed to sink from sight, but the horse swam low and fast, his wet mouth gaping with enormous teeth, his nostrils snorting for breath. When he reached our side he rose magnificently from the water and came floundering among the reeds, while the rider slid slowly out of the saddle and stood grinning in the mud.

'Ignacio,' he said. 'At your service. Do what I say and you won't get wet.'

He turned the horse round, helped me on to its back, and told me to kneel on the wooden saddle. Then he leapt up in front of me, straddling the horse's neck, and advised me to hang on to his belt.

The horse bucked and staggered among the rushes, then appeared to step into a bottomless hole. We sank deep in the river, which seemed as wide as the Congo, and headed back for the other side. The flood raced around us, tossing up pale green scum, and little waves whipped over the saddle. My boots filled with water and I felt my knees grow cold – it was like floating on top of a cupboard.

The farmer's wife was standing on the opposite bank, and she gave me her apron to dry myself. Then we walked up to the house where the farmer himself was waiting, a stiff old man in a high-crowned hat. 'Blasco Vallegas,' he said, removing his hat for a moment and holding it across his stomach. I gave him Manolo's message, at which he nodded briefly and asked me to stay to lunch.

First he showed me the farm – a structure of uncut boulders packed with clay and thatched with bulrushes.

'I built it myself,' said the farmer, 'with these very hands – when I married, forty years ago. My wife brought the stones from the Sierra on her head. Apart from herself, it was all she brought.'

He led me into the kitchen, where we sat on little chairs and drank wine out of leather cups. The room was a mazy violence of light and shade which dazzled the eyes at first, but slowly the jigsaw began to fit together and the details reveal themselves. The floor was of trodden earth, the furniture shaped by axes, and chickens perched blinking on the backs of the chairs. A pig slept in one corner, and a girl knelt in another burning her head with a lighted candle.

'My daughter,' said Blasco. 'She molests herself.'

The girl moaned 'Ay !' as though in agreement.

'She is curing a headache or some such trouble. She weighs heavily upon us all.'

He shrugged her away and poured me another cup of wine, then went to a wooden chest by the wall. He rummaged inside for a moment and returned with a pig-skin bag which he emptied upon the table.

'Look !' he said, sorting out the objects with his fingers and separating two of them. One was a small bronze figure of a naked goddess, and the other a rusty iron bracelet. He said he'd turned them up ploughing, together with other things now lost, including the jewelled tooth of a 'Moroccan Princess'.

'Do you know how long we have lived in these hills?' he asked. 'Since the very sun was made. Since before kings and altars, or the Virgin herself was a mother. Since there were leopards in the caves ...'

Vallegas didn't look like a patriarch, he was too thin and dried, but he managed to talk like one.

'Everything you see around you has come from these,' he said, holding up his hands, then striking his loins. There was the farm, and his five grown sons out working – whom I would see when it was time to eat – Ignacio with the horses, Curron down by the river, and three others up on the hill. His daughters were gracious, too – 'Except that one with the headache.' He referred to his wife as his breastbone.

But although he'd made everything, he owned nothing here – forty years working the land for others. Tomorrow might be different, he said, squinting out of the window. Tomorrow, when the 'potatoes' came.

Rocking quietly in his chair, the old man seemed to be talking to himself, recalling riots that had stirred the past – ploughing up derelict land in times of famine, soldiers coming to destroy the crops, Civil Guards on horses the size of elephants riding down the women and children. Starvation, martyrdom, jail, massacre, the slaughter of animals, homesteads burning ... The soldiers, he thought, would be on their side now; and the Civil Guard with the Devil, as usual.

As he talked, he sat stroking a piece of painted glass, a miniature portrait of the Holy Family, which he said had been tied round his neck the day he was born and which he'd carried with him ever since.

When the sons returned, we sat down to eat, and the little kitchen was crammed like a horsebox. The mother served up a pot of migas stew – a thick porridge of maize sprinkled with dried sardines, filling, but tasting of sack-cloth. Blasco ate in silence, with toothless attention, his face working like a tent in the wind, while the sons lowered their heads and ravenously gobbled, plugging their mouths with bread. It was a serious meal without conversation, the jug of wine passing formally among us. Meanwhile the women waited in the background; the mother squatting by the stove and tossing scraps of food to the pig; the girl standing behind her father, patiently watching his plate, her forehead blackened by candlesmoke.

As soon as the meal was over the men relaxed, grunting and stretching their legs. Ignacio spat on his hands and cleaned his sister's face. Another took a gun and went out to shoot partridges.

'There are many partridges here,' the youngest boy told me. 'Also rabbits, wild pig, and deer. But we may not touch the deer. They belong to the Duke.'

'To who?' barked the father.

The boy paused, open-mouthed, swallowed, and began again.

'We may touch the deer — if we can find them,' he said. 'They belong to anybody now, I think.'

The weeks leading towards summer were hot and steely, and except for the radios in the bars, crackling with political speeches, the village seemed entirely cut off from the world. The coast road to Málaga lay empty in the sun. Few people went anywhere, the air of listening returned, and the mountains moved closer like a ring of bayonets. A slow brew of expectation simmered over the houses, raising poisonous bubbles that exploded every so often in little outbreaks of irrelevant violence.

First the ice plant was sabotaged and the power station blown up — both of which belonged to a marquis. In spite of the inconvenience, everyone seemed to enjoy these gestures, and the whiff of dynamite was considered a tonic. A number of shops were looted, their windows broken, and the word BOICOT painted across the doors; a few stray priests were insulted in the streets, and a store of wine barrels rolled into the sea. Next, a group of old women went to the house of the tax collector and tossed his furniture into the street, after which they piled him and his wife on top of a cart and drove them out of town.

Then one morning the church was set on fire. 'They've done it at last!' cried Manolo. We hurried through the streets, which were full of the sweet scent of woodsmoke, and joined the villagers crowding the square. The church tower was blazing like a cardboard box, and most of the watchers seemed in a state of rapture.

I remember the faces of the fishermen, awed but beaming,

and their satisfied grunts at each burst of flame. Sensing the mood of their fathers, the children ran wild, bombarding the church with showers of stones. Only the women stayed silent, squinting sideways at their men, waiting for some stroke of doom to fall.

A week later came Feast Day, and a quick change of heart. The smoke-blackened church was filled with lilies. The images of Christ and the Virgin were brought out into the sunlight and loaded as usual on to the fishermen's backs. Anonymous, invisible, hidden beneath the embroidered drapes, they shuffled once more up and down the streets, sweating, bent double beneath their canopied burdens, the Church's traditional porters.

As the procession moved by, a peasant tore off his cap and threw himself on his knees with outspread arms.

'Holy Mother, Maria, intercede with your Son! Queen of Heaven, strike me dead! Blessed be the Virgin of Castillo, mother of the seas. Do not forsake us. Live for ever.'

It was a day of tears and breast-beating, a day of contrition. The invincible Christ had risen again – the private Christ of Castillo, scorched and defiled, yet returning to forgive his sons. Rocking, swaying, borne on rafts of wild iris, the holy images passed in triumph, preceded by the plump, red-bonneted, skirted priests, and the young girls with their trays of petals.

All was normal again. A brass band played. Rich and poor mixed their cries together. The peasants knelt with bowed heads or raised their contorted faces. 'Maria, salvame!'

Profanity, sacrilege, had been a passing madness. This was the Faith as it had always been. Then, a few days later, the church was fired again, and this time burnt to a shell.

It was now the middle of May, and tension increased in the village as the news from Madrid grew more threatening and vague. To the peasants of Castillo, the visionary promises of February seemed to have dried up in the heat. There were strikes, parades, shows of proletarian force, boys and girls marching in coloured shirts, arms raised in salute, clenched fists and slogans, painted banners and challenging speeches.

When there was a strike it was total, enforced by the police, and the fishermen picketed the sea. One saw rich old women dragging their laundry to the river, or queueing up at the village wells. At the hotel, the chambermaids sat gossiping in the sun while the chef stayed home with his wife; Herr Brandt did the cooking, wrapped in Manolo's apron, and the guests slept in unmade beds.

Each day more peasants came in from the country, massing in the square to be on hand for trouble. Many of them brought guns slung over their shoulder, sticking out of their waistbands, or tied to the saddles of donkeys – flintlocks, pistols, and old rusty muskets which might have been saved from the Peninsular War.

The split village now emerged in clearer focus and its two factions declared themselves, confronting each other at last in black and white – labelled for convenience, 'Fascist' or 'Communist'. The 'Fascists' seemed ready to accept the name, this being frankly what they aspired to, with the Falange already organized as a fighting group, a swaggering spearhead of upper-class vengeance, whose crude fascist symbols, Italian-inspired, were now appearing on walls and doorways.

The 'Communist' label, on the other hand, was too rough and ready, a clumsy reach-me-down which properly fitted no one. The farm labourers, fishermen, and handful of industrial workers all had local but separate interests. Each considered his struggle to be far older than Communism, to be something exclusively Spanish, part of a social perversion which he alone could put right by reason of his roots in this particular landscape.

In fact, I don't remember meeting an official Communist in Castillo – though 'communism' was a word in the bars. Manolo, who was a leader, had no political status at all, but was a romantic anarchist of his own invention. The local flag of revolution was the Republican flag, the flag of the elected government. The peasants strung it like a banner across the Town Hall balcony and painted their allegiance beneath it in red: 'We swear to defend this bandera with the last drop of our blood.' Sombre and ominous words.

Yet the government they supported must have seemed remote

to many, being composed entirely of middle-class politicians – without a Communist, Anarchist, or even a Socialist anywhere in its cabinet. The peasants looked to this government because their hopes lay with it, hopes they thought to realize for the first time in centuries, an opportunity to shift some of the balances which had so long weighed against them, more than against anyone else in Europe.

Spain was a wasted country of neglected land – much of it held by a handful of men, some of whose vast estates had scarcely been reduced or reshuffled since the days of the Roman Empire. Peasants could work this land for a shilling a day, perhaps for a third of the year, then go hungry. It was this simple incongruity that they hoped to correct; this, and a clearing of the air, perhaps some return of dignity, some razing of the barriers of ignorance which still stood as high as the Pyrenees.

A Spanish schoolmaster at this time knew less of the outside world than many a shepherd in the days of Columbus. Now it was hoped that there might be some lifting of this intolerable darkness, some freedom to read and write and talk. Men hoped that their wives might be freed of the triple trivialities of the Church – credulity, guilt, and confession; that their sons might be craftsmen rather than serfs, their daughters citizens rather than domestic whores, and that they might hear the children in the evening coming home from fresh-built schools to astonish them with new facts of learning.

All this could be brought about now by an act of their government and the peaceful process of law. There was nothing to stop it. Except for that powerful minority who would rather the country first bled to death.

June came in full blast, with the heat bouncing off the sea as from a buckled sheet of tin. All day in the bars the radios spat and crackled – violence in Madrid, demonstrations in Valencia, strikes and riots in Barcelona.

I met Manolo in the street on his way back from a meeting, and he laid a shaking hand on my shoulder.

'Are you going?'

'Where?'

'Home to your country.'

'No.'

'The roads are still open if you want to go.'

That morning a group of Falangists in the neighbouring village walked into a bar and shot five fishermen. The murderers, wearing arm-bands, escaped in a car to Granada. Castillo lay silent, like a shuttered camp...

In the afternoon I walked out into the country with Jacobo. Daylight nightingales were singing by the river. The air was brassy, thunderous, and only a thread of brown water ran trickling down the river bed. Some girls we knew had been gathering poppies in the field, and now they came down the path towards us, walking slowly in the heat, the red flowers wilting at their breasts, looking as though their bodies had been raked by knives.

An hour or so later we returned by another path and found two children standing under the bridge. They stood stiffly, holding hands, staring at the figure of a man who lay sprawled on the river bank. We recognized him as a local Falangist, a boy of about twenty, whose father had once been mayor. He had been shot through the head, and lay staring back at the children, flies gathering around his mouth.

# 11. War

It started in the middle of July. There were no announcements, no newspapers, just a whispering in the street and the sound of a woman weeping.

I was now living near the church, in the house of an expatriate English writer, who'd lent me a room overlooking the bay, and as I went out that morning I saw a woman lying face-down on the pavement, beating the ground with her hands. A group of neighbours stood by, making no attempt to move her – her attendants rather than comforters. They said she was weeping for her son – a young conscript in Morocco, who to her was already dead.

Down at Manolo's bar he told me what he knew; a see-saw of fact and fantasy. There had been anti-Government uprisings in the garrisons of Spanish Morocco – at Melilla, Tetuan, and Larache. On the other hand, said Manolo, there was nothing to worry about, the situation was under control ... General Francisco Franco, 'the butcher of the Asturian miners', had flown from the Canaries to lead the rebels. There were reports of other risings in Saragossa, Madrid, and Seville ... But, no, the Government had put them down ... Franco himself was dead, had been brought down in the sea, had been arrested, assassinated, shot ... Even so, Moorish troops were pouring into the south of Spain ... But they would be slaughtered before they could advance an inch ...

Indeed, there was no firm news. The café radios were silent, or jammed, or stridently at odds with each other. People gathered in the streets, staring up at the sky as though expecting to see some great proclamation written across it. And as always – impelled by the oldest instinct of the countryside – the fields emptied and peasants poured into the village, bringing their wives and children, their sheep and goats, and settling them down under the castle walls. Some of the men brought guns, but most were unarmed. They crowded the plaza, simply waiting to be used, standing with their backs to the Town Hall, shoulder to shoulder with the fishermen, as though ready to defend it with their bodies. There was no authority yet; theirs was just a defensive laager drawn up spontaneously in the face of the unknown. Meanwhile Manolo, and El Gato (the leader of one of the new-formed unions) started to organize some kind of militia.

The police had suddenly disappeared and the village was on its own: Government supporters facing the enemy within. A round of searches began among the houses of suspected 'fascists'. Manolo took men to barricade the coastal road. Then in the afternoon there arrived the first car from Málaga, driving fast and smothered with dust. It was stopped at the road-block and Manolo's bayonets surrounded it, pricking open the doors

and windows. A couple of white-faced young men were hurried off to jail, while rifles and grenades were dug out of the
boot. Later, a Frenchman drove up in a battered Fiat with a
white flag tied on the roof. He said half Málaga was in flames
and that there was fighting in the streets. He didn't know
which side was winning, or even where he was going, but he
showed us a score of bullet holes in the back of his car.

Night brought more rumours, smuggled in with the dark,
along the coast road and down from the hills. Granada was
held by the rebels, and so was our neighbour, Altofaro. The
fate of Málaga was still unknown. Meanwhile, our confused
little fortress seemed to be caught between the mountains and
the sea, with fires spreading on either side.

The militia were busy that night, determined that there
should be no rising in Castillo. The house-to-house searching of
suspects began to reveal the little caches of arms so carefully
hidden for months – packed in wine-barrels in cellars, hung in
baskets down wells, in cupboards, in clocks, up chimneys. The
loot was piled in the plaza and guarded by El Gato's militia –
the best arms they were to get in the war.

A wave of summary arrests also began that evening. Elegant
and resigned in their lacy white shirts, the young 'señoritos'
sat waiting in the paseo. When the patrols approached them,
they rose casually to their feet, crushed out their cigarettes and
strolled away under guard. The priest was rounded up too, and
I saw him brought flustered from his house and led off to jail
with the others. Few of the local 'fascists' attempted either to
escape or hide. The hour was too late for that.

'There was a plot,' said Manolo in the bar that night. 'Now
we have them tied like mules.' He looked drained, pallid, and
his face seemed to have burnt down to the wick. He knew that
bloodshed was imminent. El Gato poured him some brandy,
saying he would need it for the executions, but Manolo only
shook his head. El Gato was a large, noisy, rather teasing man,
and tonight he was drinking heavily. 'You need fire,' he said.
'You are vengeance like a trickle of ice-water.' Manolo turned
away with a ghastly smile.

These two ill-assorted men were now in control of the

village, and the bar was their headquarters – with men coming and going, raising arms in salute, bringing reports, and carrying messages. Málaga would hold, said El Gato, and if Granada attacked from the north they would find Castillo a nest of swords. Their chief concern was Altofaro, only ten miles down the coast and near enough to Africa to be used as a beachhead. If the rebels made a landing there they could out-flank Málaga from the east, and then Castillo might become the key to the war. Manolo and El Gato, having no facts to confine them, began to expand before each other's eyes, grew vast as generals, became emperors of armies, possible liberators of the entire peninsula.

Walking home after midnight, I saw a heavy guard round the prison and another round the captured arsenal. The militia were bivouacked in the street, crouching over flickering wood-fires, their faces outlined in red – high cheekbones, pitted eyes, hungry sunken cheeks, soldiers of Goya come alive again.

Early next morning, four truckloads of militia drove off to Altofaro to attack the rebels. They swung singing through the streets in their bright blue shirts, waving their caps as though going to a fair. El Gato was in charge, dynamite strapped to his body; the others shared a musket between three. Once they were over the hill, we expected to hear the sounds of war break out, but the morning passed in silence.

About noon, a white aircraft swung in low from the sea, circled the village, and flew away again – leaving the clear blue sky scarred with a new foreboding above a mass of up-turned faces. Many felt, till that moment, their village to be secure and forgotten; now the eye of war had spied them out.

Throughout the afternoon nothing happened. Families ate their meals in the street, seeking the assurance of one another's company. Once again the fierce sunlight obliterated everything it fell on, burning all colours to an ashen glare. When people stepped out of their houses they seemed to evaporate for a moment, as if the light had turned them to vapour; and when they passed into shadow they disappeared again, like stepping into a hole in the ground. That afternoon of waiting was the hottest I've known. Fear lay panting in the street like a dog. It was as though El Gato and his men had been swallowed up in silence, or had followed the war to another country.

But war was not far away, and after nightfall, unexpectedly, it paid its first mad call on Castillo. A destroyer crept into the bay, unseen by anyone, and suddenly began probing the shore with its searchlight. The beam swept over the hills, up and down the coast, and finally picked out the village and pinned it against the darkness. Held by the blazing eye, opening so ominously from the sea, the people experienced a moment of naked panic. There seemed nowhere to run to, nowhere to hide, so they hurried down to the beach, and stood motionless in the glare, facing the invisible warship and raising their arms in a kind of massed entreaty. As the searchlight played over them they remained stiffly at attention, just letting themselves be seen. In the face of the unknown, all they could do was to offer themselves in this posture of speechless acquiescence. Such pitiless brightness had never lit up their night before: friend or foe, it was a light of terror.

For a while nothing happened. The warship just sat in the darkness stroking its searchlight up and down the shore. To get a better view, I joined a group of boys who'd already climbed on to the castle wall. We could see the whole of Castillo below us – the crowds on the beach and the spoke of light turning on its invisible hub. As we watched, it began to play over the nearby hills and move again along the coastal road. Suddenly it picked out a lorry heading towards the village, then three more, all packed with men. The beam lazily followed them, as though escorting them home, lighting up their rifles like little thorns. One could hear distant shouting above the sound of the engines – it was El Gato's militia coming back at last.

The trucks roared into the village, horns stridently blowing, and pulled up in the warship's pool of light. The beam was abruptly switched off, followed by a moment of absolute darkness. Then there came a blinding flash from the sea.

Silence. It was as though a great fuse had blown. Then the mountains behind us thundered, a thunder that boomed and cannoned from peak to peak and tumbled in the valleys like showers of stones. There was another flash, another explosion, another hot blast of air. For a moment we imagined it might be some kind of salute to the militia. Then we heard the tearing scream of a shell.

The searchlight came on again. We could see the crowds on the beaches surging inland like a muddy wave. The destroyer fired once more, misting its searchlight with smoke, and we were no longer in doubt about its intentions. A house on our right suddenly shuddered, rose a foot in the air, and slowly collapsed like a puff-ball. A bundle of stones and trees leapt up by the river. A pall of dust drifted over the village.

After half a dozen more salvoes, the firing broke off; inexplicably, since we seemed to be at their mercy. Then the shocked silence in the village began to fill with a curious whispering and rustling, the sound of a multitude on the move. In the naked beam of the searchlight we saw them come stumbling up the streets, bent double, crying and moaning, mothers and fathers dragging their children behind them, old folk tottering and falling down.

As the village ran for the hills, looking for patches of darkness, we saw a small boat put out from the shore, with two squat figures inside it sitting hunched at their oars and rowing frantically towards the ship.

And that was the end of the bombardment. The destroyer was found to be friendly. It had all been an unfortunate error of war. A case of mistaken identity; the captain sent his apologies, slipped anchor, and sailed quietly away – leaving a few gaps in the houses, a few dead in the streets, and most of the population scattered across the hillsides.

When the sun rose next morning Castillo had transformed itself, with flags fluttering from every rooftop. Every scrap of old cloth within the spectrum of red, from orange, vermilion to purple, had been hastily cut into squares and run up on poles to make it clear on which side we stood. Even the houses of the 'fascists' wore scarlet that morning, as did the casino, the bank, and the church. In the face of any more trigger-happy assaults made by passing friends, it was thought as well to take no chances.

But the village seemed purged, curiously enough, by its night of fire. One heard no blame laid against the warship. In spite of the ruins and the dead, the capricious savagery of the bombardment was accepted as one of the traditional blows of fate. Castillo, if anything, felt enlarged by the ordeal; it now had wounds to boast of, had smelt the hot reek of powder, stared down the muzzle of guns, and known itself to survive. There was satisfaction, too, in the fact that the destroyer was theirs, and had splendidly shown its powers.

We learned that it was El Gato and the mayor who had stopped the shelling last night, the only ones to keep their heads. They had rowed out alone along the path of the searchlight and asked what in the hell was going on. The captain explained that he'd simply mixed up his villages and mistaken us for the rebel-held Altofaro. Moreover, he'd thought the militia were attacking, rather than returning home, and he'd only meant to help. (In fact, El Gato's expedition itself was also revealed to have been a fiasco: the men had forgotten their ammunition.)

Now that Castillo had come out under the scarlet banner, the morning was one of mounting action. This was the day when the peasants and fishermen openly took over the village, commandeering the houses of suspects and the empty villas of the rich and painting across them their plans for a new millennium. 'Here will be the Nursery School.' 'Here will be the House of Culture.' 'Here will be a Sanatorium for Women.' 'Workers, Respect this House for Agricultural Science.' 'Here will be a Training College for Girls' ... Each of the large bold words were painstakingly written in red, a memoranda of a brief and innocent euphoria. For who among the crowds could guess, as they gathered in the streets to read them, that these naïve hopes would later be treated as outrage?

Meanwhile the militia were massing for a new attack on Altofaro, undeterred by yesterday's failure. They formed up raggedly in the square, polishing their guns on their trousers and watched by a scattering of wide-eyed dogs and boys. Manolo and El Gato, in long blue overalls, marched up and down the ranks; Manolo pale and stern, El Gato loud and jovial, teasing the men with macabre jokes. The militia were mixed, some old and grizzled, others young, bright-faced, and swaggering. There was also a platoon of teenage girls armed with hand-grenades. Nobody joked with them.

About noon the militia climbed into their open lorries and rattled off up the coastal road, standing stiff and straight, arms raised in salute, calm, but not singing now. We watched the swirl of white dust climb the side of the hill and hang over the ridge in the hot still air. After they'd gone, the village was left in a kind of limbo, not knowing what to do.

I went and sat in a bar, feeling bereft and impotent, as though robbed of some great occasion. I'd seen those silent men and muscular stiff-lipped girls riding to a war just down the road, to a blaze of battle under a burning sky offering all the trappings of heroic carnage. That special adrenalin in the young which makes war easy, and welcomes it, drew me voluptuously towards Altofaro. Then why hadn't I gone? It would not have been difficult. Manolo would have arranged the thing in a moment. Even so, I hung back, as from some family affair in which I still doubted I had a part.

On the way back to the house I found Emilia, one of our neighbours, raging up and down the street. Her brother had just been arrested as a spy, and she was indulging in a public ecstasy of fury – against him, not against the authorities. She didn't doubt his guilt; he had done it for money; he was always a bestia, a sinverguenza. Here was someone at last on whom she could blame the war, someone palpable, close at home. 'Give me my brother!' she cried, opening her hands like claws, clutching and strangling the air. 'Give him to me for just a little moment, let me squeeze out his tiny life!'

Crazed and dishevelled, she ran down to the jail and beat on the bars with her fists. 'Suckler of snakes!' she shouted. 'Polluter of our mother! Give me a gun, and I'll shoot him myself!' The guards laughed at her antics but didn't turn her away; instead they quietly opened the gates. Emilia disappeared inside, and when we saw her again, an hour later, she was calmly smoking a pipe on her doorstep.

Later that afternoon we heard the sound of distant gunfire, snapping like pods in the hills. The day was dead calm and the firing came to the ears with dry little displacements of air. Then about four o'clock, two more warships appeared, steaming slowly towards the east. El Gato had boasted they'd come; he'd arranged it by radio, he said, but nobody had believed him. Now the ships moved quietly along the coast and anchored about six miles away, standing in line astern and facing the rebel port which lay just hidden behind the headland.

Once again the village crowded on to the beach to watch. The evening was hazy and peacock-coloured; delicate hues ran slowly over the sea and sky and melted together like oil. The destroyers lay low on the horizon, slender as floating leaves, insubstantial as the air around them. Lights winked, there was a glitter of sun on metal, then little flashes ran along the ships, twinkling eruptions of fire that suddenly starred the air then vanished without a sound ... The shelling of Altofaro had begun; curiously muted at first, its force softened by heat and distance. Then the sound of the explosions reached us, round and hollow, bouncing dully across the water.

The villagers watched in silence, showing no sign of excitement, but rather with a mixture of morbid compassion. Dim, muffled shudders came from behind the headland as the shells began to strike home. The bombardment continued for about an hour, then the ships steamed away, leaving a column of smoke in the air, a black greasy pall that slowly mounted the sky and spread grubbily over the twilit hills.

Long after the firing had died, and darkness fallen, the villagers still lingered along the shore, standing trance-like, rigid, strangely dumb, just staring towards the east. Once again they seemed to be tasting the fumes and the sulphur, and sensing the heat of the guns they knew, but this time the salvoes had been turned elsewhere, and the terror was in their name.

It was not victory, however; there was no victory on the coast that night. Altofaro had not been destroyed, nor had it even surrendered. When the militia returned, round about midnight, there was no singing or cheering welcome. The wounded, the shocked, the dying, and the dead were unloaded in bitter silence. Manolo was missing, and El Gato walked speechlessly away trailing his rifle like a broken limb. Something had gone wrong, something which had not been thought possible when the militia first took up arms.

Under the pale street lamps, amid the weeping and curses, the simple truth was being uncovered. After the day's massacre at Altofaro, and the clumsy impotence of the warships – whose shells appeared to have fallen harmlessly in open country – it was being learned again that men needed more than courage, anger, slogans, convictions, or even a just cause when they went to war. The village became aware that night, not for the first time in its history, that a people's army could be defeated.

The next morning they blew up the bridges on the coastal roads and so far as one could tell we were now cut off. In Castillo it was a day of nervousness and shame which led to further outbreaks of mindless violence. As I walked down to the café to get news of Manolo, I saw that the casino had been sacked and burnt.

It had been a cheap, florid building, pseudo-Moorish in style, but nevertheless a symbol of civic pride. Now the villagers had set upon it and savagely torn it to pieces, in spite of their love of its gaudy grandeur. By the time I arrived, it was already a littered ruin, a black and degraded mess. Men and women stood around it, sniffing the curling smoke and kicking at broken pieces of furniture : out in the street a grand piano lay with its legs in the air, smouldering gently like a roasted ox; and an air of orgiastic gloom pervaded the scene, a sour and desolate sadness.

The militia were utterly demoralized. There was no more talk of returning to the offensive or of making another attack on Altofaro. The lorries baked in the sun, and throughout the long afternoon the men squabbled or simply slept.

Later that night Manolo returned, having made his way back along the coast on foot. He walked quietly into the bar like an apparition, his face drawn, his clothes dripping with sea-water.

El Gato, who had been drinking and dozing all evening, rose to his feet with a grunt and embraced him.

They stood, the two leaders, the big and the small, holding on to each other stiffly.

'Where were you?' asked El Gato. 'We didn't mean to leave you, man. We had to get out, you understand.'

Manolo nodded.

'I saw you go,' he said. 'I buried myself. Isidro was lying just across the alley. He was still alive when they found him and they cut his throat. When it got quiet, I went into the sea.'

'Is the bridge down?'

'Yes. I swam to the Faro – then I came on over the cliff.'

'What about the ships?'

'You saw them. You saw what they did.'

'Can we get back?'

'Not with this gang, never.'

El Gato gave Manolo some brandy, then stripped off his cartridge belt and tossed it into a corner. An air of absolute exhaustion settled down on the bar. 'We're finished before we started,' said Manolo. His companions sat round in silence staring at the blank bare walls. El Gato went to sleep again.

About midnight, we got through to Radio Sevilla, and heard Queipo de Llano exulting in the fall of the city. The rebel general was drunk, and each slurred, belching phrase was a slap in the face of the militia. Christ had triumphed, he ranted, through God's army in Spain, of which Generalissimo Franco was the sainted leader. The criminal forces of socialism, which had drawn their slime across the country, were being routed by the soldiers of righteousness. He ordered the workers to submit and to return to work, otherwise they and their families would be shot. God's army was merciful, but Spain would be emptied if necessary. 'Viva España! Viva la Virgen!'

'It's true,' said Manolo, shivering with fever and struggling to keep awake. The rebels were steadily building up their forces from Africa, he said; flying in thousands of Moorish troops each day. 'The Catholic kings were the first to drive the Moors from Spain. Now the Catholic generals are bringing them back.

What can we do? There's nothing to stop them. The war is over, I think.'

Walking home that night, I was not to know that Manolo was wrong, and that the long war was only just beginning. Nor did I know, as I went to bed, that I had only a few hours left in Spain.

When I awoke next morning there was yet another warship in the bay, swinging gently at anchor in the sunshine. It rode sleepily on the water, deck-awnings in place and with its guns reassuringly covered. Taking breakfast on the terrace with my English friend, we watched it idly over the tops of the palm trees. There seemed to be no movement on board, and the village itself lay hazed in a silence which promised another hot and hooded day.

Then we heard a rush of footsteps in the street, a loud hammering on the door, and the house was invaded by women and children, who came stumbling up the stairs, excitedly calling our names and led by a flushed and dishevelled Emilia.

'Hurry!' she cried. 'Leave everything – you are saved! Your king has sent you a ship. They are waiting for you on the beach and have come to take you home. Before God, who more fortunate than you?'

They dragged me out of the house and hurried me down to the shore, urging me on with impatient shouts. 'Run, run, Lorenzo! Your friend the admiral is waiting!' The women were skipping around me like frogs.

Sure enough, a ship's cutter was drawn up on the sand, guarded by pink-cheeked British sailors. A smart officer in white, who had been making inquiries at the hotel, strolled down the steps and introduced himself.

No panic, he said, but the Navy had sent out a destroyer from Gibraltar to pick up any British subjects who might be marooned on the coast. Could we be ready in an hour? The situation was edgy. Alas, personal baggage only...

So it had come – the sudden end to my year's adventure, with the long arm reaching from home, the destroyer bobbing in the bay like an aproned nanny, the officer like a patient elder brother. Responsible, tolerant, but slightly bored, he was here to snatch us from alien perils, to honour the birthright inscribed in our passports, and to stop us making fools of ourselves.

Naturally, he said, it was up to us. We could stay and sweat it out if we wished. But he couldn't guarantee they'd be back, and the Civil War was spreading. His captain advised us to get out now.

I knew I would have to go. I couldn't resist the flattery of the occasion – all the paraphernalia of official rescue, so lavishly gathered and waiting, and the villagers' expectations as they crowded around us. As much as anything else it was their faces which decided me, faces already set for a huge farewell. The King of England had sent a ship for the hotel fiddler and his friend, and our departure was a dramatic necessity.

Castillo was a trap in any case, and I'd been looking for other ways out, plotting to join a fishing boat to Málaga or Africa. But fantasies of private action were now swamped by the benevolent presence of the Navy. I went back to the house and began to collect my things.

The novelist was already packed, with a crate of books and papers, some roots of asphodel and a barrel of coñac. Emilia and her neighbours were engaged in fighting their way through the house, helping themselves to the sheets and furniture, weeping as they did so and occasionally throwing their arms around us and saying what a hole we should leave in their lives.

Finally a large happy crowd, loudly bewailing our departure, escorted the pair of us down to the beach, dumped our goods in the water, begged us not to leave them, and lifted us bodily into the boat. The sailors jumped in after us, not a moment too soon, and we were off, launched by a hundred hands. A young friend of the novelist, with a desperate cry, flung himself into the sea behind us, swam a few wild strokes in sobbing pursuit, and then allowed his companions to drag him back to shore.

It was over, finished – the hoarse echoes of Spain slowly dying away in the distance. We headed for the destroyer, which loomed gradually larger, a new and dominating presence; but looking back at Castillo receding in the hard blue sunlight we saw its outlines transformed. The white houses, grey sands, silver and orange rocks were blackened with a multitude of watchers. The whole village had turned out to witness our departure and stood in a long dark frieze round the bay, waving and calling across the water, some of them running up and down the sands. There was also something desperate, almost sinister, in the way they packed the edge of the sea, as though in dread of the land behind them.

We reached the waiting destroyer, and were piped briskly aboard to a line-up of saluting officers – an engaging, solemn, and unexpected little ritual which gracefully ignored our down-at-heel appearance. I saw my small bits of baggage passed hand-to-hand up the gangway and piled politely on the quarter deck. The captain welcomed us with a handshake like a squire at a picnic. Room was made for us in the junior officers' cabins.

Once we were safely aboard, the ship leapt into life and sliced in a fast sharp curve out to sea – a multi-million pound vessel, throbbing with power, manned by a hundred and thirty crew, its engines burning up fuel at £X a minute, and all for a couple of English tramps. It was midday now, with the deck awnings flapping and the starch-blue sea racing by, the officers wandering below for their pre-lunch drinks, and the novelist already typing . . .

But I stayed on deck, watching Castillo grow small and Spain folding itself away – all its clamour gone, wrenched so abruptly from me, a year's life in a few hours ended. I saw the long hard coast, which I'd trodden inch by inch, become a clinker of bronze on the skyline. Behind it the peaks of the Sierras crawling jaggedly into view, hung there suspended, then fell away – and in that instant of leaving them I felt them as never before, clutching at my senses like hands of bone. From that seaborne distance, cut off and secure, I seemed only then to begin to know that country; could smell its runnels of dust, the dead ash of its fields, whiffs of sour wine, rotting offal, and incense, the rank hide of its animals, the peppery skin of its men, the sickly tang of its fevered children.

I saw again, as I lost them, the great gold plains, the arid and mystical distances, where the sun rose up like a butcher each morning and left curtains of blood each night. I could hear the talk, the cries, the Spanish-Arabic voices pitched to carry from Sierra to Sierra; the trickling sound of guitars dropping like water on water, eroding the long boredom of afternoons; and the songs, metallic, hatcheting the ear, honed with forlorn and unattainable lusts; the strangled poetry of the boys, the choked chastity of the girls, and the orgasmic outbursts of tethered beasts.

All I'd known in that country – or had felt without knowing it – seemed to come upon me then; lost now, and too late to have any meaning, my twelve months' journey gone. Spain drifted away from me, thunder-bright on the horizon, and I left it there beneath its copper clouds.

An officer came up on deck and handed me a drink. 'Shame to break up your holiday like this,' he said. Later, a German airship passed above us, nosing inquisitively along the coast, the swastika black on its gleaming hull. To Spain, so backward and so long ignored, the nations of Europe were quietly gathering.

# 12. Epilogue

Back in England it was August, bank holiday time, with the country deep in the grip of a characteristic mid-Thirties withdrawal, snoozing under old newspapers and knotted handkerchiefs.

I returned to my Gloucestershire village, amazed to see once more the depth of the grass and the weight of the leaves on the trees. But the pleasure of being home again, and receiving the traditional cosseting of the prodigal, was quickly replaced by misgivings. I'd been away two years, but was little the wiser for it. I was twenty-two, woolly-minded, and still naïve in everything, but I began to realize I'd come home too soon.

The Spanish War, seen close to within the local limits of an Andalusian village, was not what it had seemed to me at the time. As I learnt more about it from the newspapers – its scale and implications – I couldn't help feeling a private sense of betrayal.

Unlike so many of my age, for whom Spain in the Thirties represented one of the last theatres of political romanticism, I hadn't consciously chosen it as a Cause but had stumbled on it by accident, simply by happening to be there. Now I began to feel shameful doubts at having turned my back on events so easily, just when they were about to affect us all. I thought the least I could do was to give myself a second chance by returning to Spain as soon as I could.

It was a restless summer. I was penniless, without contacts, and totally ignorant of ways and means. Spain was over a thousand miles away and already sealed off by the hypocrisies of non-intervention. I might have given up the idea if I hadn't suddenly fallen in love, but the result of that experience, which went deeper than anything I'd known before, only made my situation all the more intolerable.

For me it was an hallucination of honour, no doubt a self-indulgence, irrelevant to events and certainly irrelevant to the girl. I told her my plans one evening as she sat twisting her hair with her fingers and gazing into my eyes with her long cat look. She wasn't impressed. Others may need a war, she said; but you don't, you've got one here. She bared her beautiful small teeth and unsheathed her claws. Heroics like mine didn't mean a thing. If I wished to command her admiration by sacrificing myself to a cause she herself was ready to provide one.

Of course, I tried to persuade her that I would be doing it for her, but this wasn't true, and she knew it. All the same, it was partly our entanglement that drove me, the feeling of over-indulgence and satiety brought on by too much easy and unearned pleasure. Guilt, too: she was married and had two young children, she was rich and demandingly beautiful, extravagantly generous with her emotions but fanatically jealous, and one who gave more than she got in love. For several days and nights our arguments swung back and forth, interspersed with desperate embraces, ending with threats of blackmail and bitter tears, with cries of 'Go, and you'll see me no more . . .'

With the help of another friend, I left London in the autumn and worked my way down through France, heading in the direction of the Pyrenees, planning, when the chances were right, simply to walk into the mountains and slip across the frontier alone. The Pyrenees, when I got there, were already touched with snow and looked grey and impregnable. Even so, I never doubted that I could get across. Winter was closing in like a cloak.

While I was waiting near the coast and making some rather slip-shod preparations, the girl suddenly turned up again, having driven out from England not in an attempt to dissuade me further but to present me instead with a week of passionate farewell. A week of hysteria, too – embracing in ruined huts, on the salt-grass at the edge of the sea, gazing out at the wind-swept ocean while gigantic thunderstorms wheeled slowly round the distant mountains.

There were no more questions or arguments; the mountains were always in sight, and the girl made it clear she thought I was going to my death. Our love was more violent than ever, as though we accepted this as its end and wished to leave each other destroyed.

After we parted, I moved on to the little town of Perpignan only about twelve miles from the Pyrenees. Perpignan, I'd been told, was swarming with Spanish Government agents eager to recruit volunteers and smuggle them over the mountains. Certainly the agents were there, but they must have thought me a doubtful proposition for my approaches were either blocked or met by evasions. When I mentioned the International Brigade, the Spanish Consul was polite and said he had no knowledge of such a body. He appreciated my goodwill but assured me that he ran no excursions across the frontier: such junketings would be unthinkable and lawless. The war was a domestic matter, he said, and everything was going well; but if I really wished to help I should go back home.

I spent a couple of weeks in the town without breaking through this wall of equivocation, and finally I realized I would have to go it alone. The Pyrenees to the south, seen in the sharp winter air, began to look smaller and less non-committal. So early in December I took a bus to Ceret in the foothills, where I spent my last snug night in an inn. Then next morning, at first light, I left the still sleeping village and started off up the mountain track.

Behind me, as I climbed, the gentle slopes of the foothills fell away to Perpignan and the sea, while before me the steep bulk of the Pyrenees Orientales filled the sky with their sunlit peaks. I had about eight hours of daylight but was not too sure of my route, except that it must go up, over, and south. The fact that it was winter seemed to be the only thing in my favour, though I was still glad of the bright clear weather.

The track rose steeply among rocks that were diamond-crusted with ice, and I soon found the going tough. I was idiotically equipped for such a journey, having brought nothing that would help me, though plenty of stuff that wouldn't – no maps, no compass, no tent or ground-sheet, instead a rucksack loaded down with an assortment of books and papers, together with my violin, a folding camera, and a saucepan. I don't really know why I was carrying all this, except that it was all I had in the world.

Throughout the long clear morning I struggled up the mountain path, buffeted by icy winds from the north. The great peak of Canigou stood away on my right, floating in the brilliant sky like an iceberg, and for much of the time, not having a compass, I was able to use it as a sighting post. By noon I'd climbed to about 3,000 feet, but the goat track grew more and more tortuous, so I decided to abandon it altogether and go straight up the mountain, still keeping Canigou on my right.

The way was tricky and hard, and I found myself stumbling on my knees and clawing at rocks and tufts of frozen grass. By the middle of the afternoon I was sweating in the cold, slipping and scrambling over the broken slopes. But I was high up now, with a prickling across the back of my neck as I felt the whole of France plunging away behind me. Having been born and brought up at two hundred and fifty feet above sea-level, I was not used to such dizzying elevations.

Suddenly there was an ominous change in the atmosphere, an extra keenness of cold, and a curious glare and whitening of the sunlight. Looking down, I saw that the foothills had disappeared and had been replaced by a blanket of swirling vapour. The shining peak of Canigou began to switch on and off like a lighthouse, intermittently shuttered by racing clouds. Then the wind rose abruptly to a thin-edged wail, and I felt the first stinging bite of snow.

One moment I'd been climbing a mountain in a sparkle of sunshine; the next, the whole visible world had gone, and I was slapped to my knees and pinioned to a shelf of rock, head down in a driving gale. Gusts of snow swept round me, needling into my eyelids and piercing my clothes like powdered glass. The storm closed in and began scouring the mountain with an insane and relentless frenzy.

For a while I curled myself up and became just a ball of survival, mindlessly hugging the lee of a rock. I lay knee to chin, letting the storm ride over me; then I began to wonder what I was doing here. After all the boasting I'd done in summer fields back home, and in her Chanel-scented bed, what was I doing in France stuck to the face of a mountain alone in a winter blizzard? To lie freezing to death on the wrong side of the frontier was no way to go to a war. There was no point in staying where I was, so I started to move forward, crawling slowly on hands and knees. Distance, direction, movement, and balance were all fused by the driving snow; I may have advanced half a mile, or just a few yards, there was no longer any way of knowing. All I remember is the brightness of the ground, and being swept by waves of almost infantile pleasure, the delirious warmth of impending frostbite.

Then, by one of those long-shot chances, taken for granted at the time, I came upon a rough little stone-built shelter. It was

half in ruins, and there was nothing inside it but straw, but I
suppose it may have saved my life. Once I'd bedded myself
down, I heard the blizzard change gear, rising to an almost
supersonic shriek, and for a couple of hours I lay motionless,
curled deep in the straw, slowly and painfully thawing out.

Later it grew dark, and the anguish gradually eased as I built
up a drowsy fug for myself. The sound of the wind settled
down to a steady whine, soporific, like an electric motor. A
pleasant comfort crept over me; I seemed to sense the feather-
soft snow gathering in deep weightless drifts outside; a bosomy
presence, invisible and reassuring, cushioning the naked rocks
of the mountain. By now I was exhausted anyway, too drugged
by the cold to move, even to attempt to build a fire; so I just
lay, sniffing the damp warm smell of the straw, and presently I
fell asleep.

Next morning the storm was over and the sun shone brilli-
antly again. I came out of the dark little hut to find the mountain transformed – trees, rocks, and bushes thickly bolstered
with snow and giving off a clean crispy smell, like starch. The
French village below me was no longer in sight, but the slope
above curved gradually away, smooth and bright, rising a few
hundred yards then ending in a sharp blue line of sky.

Abandoning the cosy gulley where I'd spent the night, I
climbed unsteadily for an hour or so, ploughing through snow-
drifts, stumbling over hidden rocks, and slithering about in my
sodden shoes. It was a long cold struggle, and I'd had nothing to
eat, but at least I was lucky to be on the move at all. Then
suddenly there was no more climbing; the slope levelled and
stopped, the sky plunged, and I was on top of the ridge.

The icy crests of the Pyrenees stretched east and west, flashing in the sun like broken glass on a wall, while before me, to
the south, was what I had come to see – range after range of
little step-like hills falling away to the immensities of Spain . . .

But I was not over the mountains yet; there was still another
ridge to cross, with a deep valley lying between. I could see a
black frozen stream winding a thousand feet below me. I
would simply have to go down and up again.

Crossing this mile-wide chasm took me the rest of the day –

a vertical, trackless journey. Whipped by flurries of snow and bruising winds I slithered, slipped, and scrambled, seeing no living thing except a boy and a sheepdog who both fled when they saw me coming. Towards evening, very cold, and with a rime of frost on my eyelashes, I was about half-way up the second slope, when I came to a small mountain road, the first I'd seen for two days, winding bleakly among the trees. I sat and stared at it for a while, but it told me nothing; it could have been anywhere on earth – just an inscrutable little cart-track, half mud, half stones, as nameless as a peasant's face.

But darkness was coming now, and I was limp with hunger. I didn't fancy another night on the mountain. So I thought I'd better follow the road and see where it led me, even if it meant a clash with the frontier guards. The track wound upwards for half a mile through a thicket of pine trees and presently emerged in a little clearing. I saw roof-tops, a church, and a cluster of village lights. Then I smelt hot butter, and knew I was still in France.

Except for a hobbled horse and a couple of snarling dogs, the village street was empty. The low wooden houses, crudely thatched with bracken, had a look of dark Siberian squalor; but half-way up the street I saw the lights of a café shining warmly through steamed-up windows. I pushed open the door and entered a noisy room full of little men in sheep's-wool coats. But when they saw me they froze as though I'd let in a blast of snow, and their conversation switched off abruptly.

What rough beast was this slouching towards the bar, dressed in a blanket and crumpled hat, coming out of the night like some ghost of winter, his hair and eyebrows white with frost? Nobody moved or spoke, except the old woman behind the bar who bobbed quickly out of sight as I approached her, and whose place was immediately taken by a huge-bellied man who began setting up bottles like a defensive wall.

I asked if I could have something to eat, and he repeated the question to the room, then, after a pause, nodded to an empty table. I slumped down in the chair, and presently he brought me some soup, which seemed to be a mixture of tar and onions. As I ate, the men watched me – rows of bright little faces wrapped to the ears in their fleece-lined collars. Some quietly shuffled their dominoes, others winked cryptically at one other, all seemed to be waiting for something to happen.

At last a committee of three detached themselves from the rest and came over and sat at my table. They were low-voiced and confidential, and one of them offered me a cigarette. I didn't have to answer, but they'd rather like to know : what exactly was I doing here? I'd come from Perpignan, hadn't I? I'd been seen there several times recently; also down in Ceret, a couple of days ago. It was hard on the mountain at this time of the year. I mustn't mind their curiosity.

They were a strange little trio but seemed harmless enough. One of them wore the look of a sleepy clown; the other had a Karl Marx beard, extravagantly bushy and white; the third was thin, like a weathered pole. But the warmth of the room, the soup, and their polite concern encouraged me to take a chance. I told them I was on my way to the 'south'. I had friends there, I said – I wanted to join them, that was all. They asked a few more questions, then the fat clown smiled. 'Well, since you've got this far . . .' he said. He called for some brandy and poured me a glass. 'Drink it up, man. You're going to need it.'

I was lucky. It might just as easily have gone the other way, with an ignominious return to Perpignan. But it seemed I'd fallen on my feet among the very men who could help me : a cosy community of frontier anarchists. I don't know why they decided to trust me, or why they thought me worth the trouble, but clearly they'd made up their minds. The men put their heads together and held a brief discussion, then the thin one looked at his watch and nodded. 'It'll take us an hour,' he said, 'so as soon as you're ready. Better go before the moon comes up.'

He rose to his feet and wrapped a scarf round his long thin neck as though he was lagging a water pipe. The others helped me on with my bags and I was given some more brandy for the journey. The proprietor refused to be paid for the soup. Then the thin man said 'Come', and pushed open the door to admit a flurry of powdered snow, and we left the café to a murmur of benevolent farewells and a flourish of political salutes.

Once in the street, my companion glanced quickly at the sky, put out his cigarette, and rolled up his collar. 'Stay close, and say nothing,' he muttered briefly, then shot off up a narrow lane. I hurried after him, and we were out of the village immediately, climbing a steep and brutish path. The man raced on ahead of me, taking little goat-like leaps and dodging nimbly from rock to rock. I could see his tall gaunt figure bouncing against the hazy stars. He never bothered to check that I was still behind him.

Easy enough for him, I thought: he was built for these mountains while I'd been raised on very low hills. His legs were long and mine were short – I was also carrying a twenty-pound load. I did my best to keep with him but he soon outstripped me and I started to fall farther and farther back. I wanted to shout, 'Wait a minute!' but it didn't seem to be the thing to do. Instead, I began to indulge in a bit of carefree whistling.

That stopped him in the end. I found him perched on a rock waiting impatiently for me to catch up. 'Stop whistling,' he growled. 'Save it for the other side. This is no time for trivialities.' At least I was grateful for the halt, and the conversation. I asked him if he did this often. I must be mad, he said; it was the very first time, and by God he was sorry already.

He started climbing again while I went panting behind him, sweat trickling down my arms and legs. Brittle gusts of dry snow swept by on the wind, striking the face like handfuls of rice. I felt engulfed by a contest that was growing too large for me; something I'd asked for but doubted that I could carry through. My companion ignored this, pushing ahead more relentlessly than ever, as though wishing to put me to the final test. That last half-hour was perhaps the worst I've known, casually unprepared as I was; ill-shod, badly clothed, and lumbered with junk, clawing my way up these icy slopes.

The point of collapse must have been near, but luckily I escaped it, for at last we reached the top of the rise. We were in a narrow pass flanked by slabs of rock which stood metallic and blue in the starlight. I seemed to sense a change in the air, a curious lifting of pressure before me as though some great obstacle had been rolled away. There was also a faint smell of charcoal, woodsmoke, and mules, and an indefinable whiff of pepper. My guide drew me into the shadows and gestured me to silence, sticking out his neck and sniffing the sky. We crouched in the darkness listening. We heard the wind, falling water, and what sounded like a distant gunshot.

'This is where I leave you,' said the Frenchman. He appeared a little more cheerful now. 'The frontier is between those rocks. Follow the path for half a kilometre and you'll come to a little farm. Knock on the door and you'll be among your friends.'

Suddenly it seemed too simple – after weeks of speculation and doubt, and these last two exhausting days – just a gap in the rocks a few hundred yards ahead of me, the tiny frontier between peace and war.

'Move slow and easy. There may be a few guards about but they shouldn't be too lively on a night like this. If you're challenged, drop everything and run like hell. Good luck, then; I can do no more.'

But there was no opposition. I just walked towards the rocks and slipped between them as though on an evening stroll. A narrow path led downwards among the boulders. Then, after about half a kilometre, just as the Frenchman had said, I saw a little farmhouse and knocked on the door. It was opened by a young man with a rifle who held up a lantern to my face. I noticed he was wearing the Republican armband.

'I've come to join you,' I said.

'*Pase usted*,' he answered.

I was back in Spain, with a winter of war before me.

# More about Penguins and Pelicans

*Nina Bawden*

## Anna Apparent

'Miss Bawden's polished story-telling rarely lets her down in this sensitive appraisal of somewhat raffish middle-class people being horrid to each other' – *Sunday Telegraph*

'Miss Bawden's novel is a corker . . . masterpieces of comic insight' – Auberon Waugh

'Her writing is sharp, witty, meticulous and it never flags' – *London Evening Standard*

## A Woman of My Age

'Nina Bawden is an artist,' as the *Sunday Times* has stated. As she deftly welds Elizabeth's half-remembered past with the shattering realities of the present – deceit, adultery and death – 'the portrait that emerges of an intelligent woman in wedlock is as true as it is sharp' – *The Times Literary Supplement*

## The Birds on the Trees

Nina Bawden has an uncanny ear for the foibles, jargon and petty vanities of the members of a family. Sympathetically, yet acutely, she shows how the generation gap widens with every frenzied effort to close it . . .

# Dear Me
*Peter Ustinov*

'Mr Ustinov's own memory is both abundant and imaginative: hence *Dear Me*, a controversial autobiography, bursting at the seams with uproarious stories, wise saws and modern instances, and ablaze with images' – J. W. Lambert in the *Sunday Times*

'There are actually six Peter Ustinovs, and I admire them all: actor, author, designer, director, film star, playwright . . . Their latest contribution, *Dear Me*, is the minaret gracing their careers, which appear – thank Fortune – to have no end in sight' – Garson Kanin

# The Country Railway
*David St John Thomas*

For those who regret the passing of Britain's country railways, this loving portrayal will bring back the charm and nostalgic delight of that halcyon time when rural branch lines were a necessary and much appreciated lifeline for people living in country outposts. Trim station platforms, colourful gardens, tank engines' shining brasswork, daringly built viaducts, decorative bridges and embankments carpeted with flowers – all these features are celebrated in words and pictures in this unique labour of love.

# Dylan Thomas
*Paul Ferris*

'A hilarious, shocking, sad story. Mr Ferris has sifted through a great mass of material, written and oral, and assembled his findings with outstanding care and skill. This is a brilliant book' – Kingsley Amis in the *Observer*

'Mr Ferris has marshalled all the facts with exemplary skill and his comments on them are always intelligent and perceptive. His Portrait of the Artist as a Bad Egg is an excellent piece of work' – Francis King in the *Sunday Telegraph*

*Recent and forthcoming Penguins*

# A Boy at the Hogarth Press
*Richard Kennedy*

Richard Kennedy started work at the Hogarth Press when he was sixteen. This account of his experiences there is described by John Lehmann as 'absolutely accurate and hilariously funny'. It provides a delightful glimpse into the everyday comings and goings of the Bloomsbury Group and an affectionate recollection of Leonard and Virginia Woolf at work: and, like Lely's portrait of Cromwell, it shows them 'warts and all'.

# In Vogue
*Georgina Howell*

*In Vogue* builds up a composite picture of the woman, year by year, from her hair to her shoes, to her scent, her stance and the cut of her clothes. Here too are the women who wore the clothes – Theda Bara, Lady Diana Cooper, Vivien Leigh, Jean Shrimpton, Twiggy – the designers who dressed them – Poiret, Chanel, Dior, Mary Quant, Saint Laurent – and the artists who projected the image – Beaton, Horst, Bailey, Eric, and Bouché.

'Captured for ever . . . the mood of a million moments in one volume' – *Daily Mail*

# The Book of Cats
*Edited by George MacBeth and Martin Booth*

P. G. Wodehouse's Webster, Saki's Tobermory, Kipling's Cat that Walked by Himself, Eliot's Macavity, Don Marquis' mehitabel: short stories from Patricia Highsmith, Roy Fuller, and Giles Gordon: the classics of Walter de la Mare, W. W. Jacobs, and Edgar Allan Poe: paintings by Goya, Picasso, Chagall, Hockney, and Douanier Rousseau: in all an affectionate medley of prose, poem and picture in praise of that most elusive and fascinating creature – the cat.

*Laurie Lee*

# Cider With Rosie

'This poet, whose prose is quick and bright as a snake
... a gay, impatient, jaunty and in parts slightly mocking
book; a prose poem that flashes and winks like a prism'
– H. E. Bates in the *Sunday Times*, London

*Cider With Rosie* puts on record the England that was
traded for the petrol engine. Recalling life in a remote
Cotswold village nearly forty years ago, Laurie Lee
conveys the semi-peasant spirit of a thousand-years-old
tradition.

First published in the United States under the title
*Edge of Day: Boyhood in the West of England*